Firefighter War Stories III

BOOKS BY LEW LEBLANC

War Stories:

    Some Memories from the Firehouse Years

Firefighter War Stories II:

    More Memories from the Firehouse Years

Firefighter War Stories III:

    Some Early Memories & The Firehouse Years

Firefighter War Stories III
Some Early Memories & The Firehouse Years

Lew LeBlanc

Edited by Sue LeBlanc

ATP
2022

Copyright © 2022 by Lew LeBlanc

Edited and Photoshopped by Sue LeBlanc

Drawings by Maya Joniaux

All rights reserved. This book or any portion thereof may not be reproduced or transmitted in any form or by any means, electrical or mechanical, including photocopying, recording, or by an information storage and retrieval system—except for the use of brief quotations in a book review or scholarly journal—without the express written permission of the publisher.

Although the author and publisher have made every effort to ensure the accuracy and completeness of information contained in this book, we assume no responsibility for errors, inaccuracies, omissions, or any inconsistency herein. All opinions expressed in this book are those of the author.

Andremily Tree Publishing, Natick, Massachusetts

FirefighterWarStories@verizon.net

Printed and bound in the United States of America

First Printing: 2022

First edition, Georgia font, 12 pt.

ISBN 978-0-578-26334-2

Dedication

This work is dedicated to the men and women of the fire service everywhere, who do the job every day because they love it: greatest job in the world.

Contents

Acknowledgements i
Preface iii
Introduction 1

The Stories:
    Doing It Right 5
    Put on Those Eggs and Hammie, Mammie! 7
    Some Brush Fires 8
    Rising from the Dead 10
    Confined Space 12
    The Night New York Was Closed 15
    Test of Time 16
    Loose Moose 18
    Irony 19
    Some Winter Memories 21
    Bad Timing 23
    Big Bad John 25
    Someday 28
    What If I Had Listened? 29
    Halloween Memory 31
    Oh Boy… 33
    No Gazelles 35
    Birthday Tours 37
    I Wasn't There 39
    Dropping the Eves 40

Mountain Memories 41

We've Come a Long Way, Baby 43

Cutting Costs 45

Coffee…Our Life's Blood 47

Some Nasty Shit 49

The Black Hole 51

Rocket Man 53

He Wasn't Worried 55

Who's the Teacher? 56

Lividity 60

Oops… 61

Learning Never Stops 63

Sticking Around 66

Keeping the Job 67

Number Please 70

Memory Lapse 72

People 74

Lamont 76

He Sank the Navy 78

Technology Confusion 79

The Phantom 82

An Unwelcome Change 83

Look Before You Leap 87

A Sight to Be Remembered 88

Eeewwwwww! 90

Keys 91

Uniforms 93

Had It Been Another Day	96
The White Wave of Death	98
Tools of the Trade	99
Ahhhhh, the Chiefs	100
One in Ten Thousand	105
What the Hell Was That?	107
The Bus	108
Just Do Your Job	110
Wow...Just Wow...	112
Robots	113
Police Matter	114
A Better Way	116
The Passenger	118
Got Him	119
Couldn't Be Me	121
Old Station 1	123
Fund Raising	126
For a Day in the Sun	128
Parade Rest	130
A Nicer Shade of Green	131
Your Life Depends on It	132
Specialists	134
Those Ch Ch Ch Changes	136
My Last Officers' Meeting	138
Gravity Calls	141
Of Funeral Homes and Beyond	142
Where the Hell is That?	144

Always a Target	146
Hearing the Voices	147
Strange Happenings (Screams in the Night)	149
Exam Time	151
The Right Tools Make the Job Easier	156
Drivers	157
Vermin	159
It's a Small Town Thing	160
A Glow in the Darkness	162
Geography Lesson	165
Worth the Price of Admission	166
Not on *My* Lawn!	167
Not on *My* Lawn, Either!	168
The Bronk	170
Harsh Justice	171
No Brother of Mine	173
Mom	175
New Apparatus	177
The Emerald Forest	179
Driving Exploits	181
And So It Begins	182
WTF	183
A Ghost from the Past	184
Info Unlooked For	186
Spy Among Us	188
It Was All Good…Almost	190
Sheets	195

Banzai	197
Hells o'Hammer!	200
Bull's Eye	202
Great Place to Train	203
A Night Always Remembered	205
Getting to the Bottom of Things	208
The Great Melee	209
It Could Always Be Worse	212
Buried Treasure	214
A Gift of Love	215
Why We Test	216
Old Homestead Fire	217
My Man	219
Holy Shit	221
Time Marches On	223
Some Thoughts	226
Glossary	**227**

Acknowledgements

To all my former students, classmates, brothers and sisters in the fire service, friends all, who read and enjoyed many of my stories and encouraged me to put them together into a book, I give my sincerest thanks.

To Sue: my partner, assistant, editor, critic, wife, and best friend; I can never thank you enough. Without your love, help, and encouragement this work would never have gotten done.

Preface

Well, you dared to wish it and now it's come true! Book number three in the Firefighter War Stories trilogy is done. I dug a little deeper in my memory and found a wealth of stories just asking to be told.

My first two books, <u>War Stories: Some Memories from the Firehouse Years</u> and <u>Firefighter War Stories II: More Memories from the Firehouse Years</u>, told tales of fires and rescues, side jobs and station life. This newest work has all of that plus more.

I grew up in the same small town that I worked in for more than thirty years. I saw a lot of changes as the town grew. I took the liberty of including some of those memories in this book.

Enjoy!

Lew

Introduction

Having worked in the fire service and fire training for more than thirty years, I guess it's no real surprise that in addition to living the life, I also like to read about it. In my personal library, I have stories of just about every disastrous fire and calamity that has ever happened in modern times. The collection is growing all the time. I also have books about careers, as well as the life and times in the fire service, written by those who lived and worked it.

One of the first books I got many years ago was Dennis Smith's <u>Report from Engine Co. 82</u>, a great work about firefighting in the South Bronx in the late 60s and early 70s. I am fortunate enough to have a copy of <u>Ready to Roll...Ready to Die</u> by retired District Chief Paul F. Cook of the Boston fire department, autographed to me by the author. Who can speak of books from the Boston fire department without bringing up the name of Leo D. Stapleton, retired chief and commissioner? I am very fortunate to also have an autographed copy of his first work, <u>Thirty Years on the Line</u>, covering happenings during his long career in the city of Boston. Mr. Stapleton has written many other works as well, and I have several of these in my collection.

I am a lover of nonfiction, so when I shop for reading material, I look carefully for what is available. Fictional stories about fires and the fire service abound. Maybe I'll read them after I finish all the nonfiction stories. Perhaps I'm just looking in the wrong places, but I have not run across stories from the smaller, suburban fire departments.

A fire is the same no matter where it burns. Some are bigger...much bigger, but they are still fires. The type of person who takes the job of firefighter is the same anywhere you go. Of course, you have some who just want it said that they are firefighters and love to wear the uniform. You get that element with any group. But the men and women who look for this job, this kind of life because they love it, are a unique breed. They live and work together. They socialize together. Everywhere they go, they "talk shop." A firefighter from anywhere can walk into a firehouse anywhere else and be greeted as a brother or sister and feel like they're home. They are part of a culture that has to be lived to be truly understood. It's easy to tell fire stories to a group of firefighters. When firefighters tell stories with one another, they all speak the same language and use the same jargon.

Once I had retired, I found myself out in the world much more than I had been during my thirty-something years on the job. I had to learn to talk to non-fire people again. I got better at it. Like many people, I started using social media on my computer. I found very many old friends and classmates, many who were not involved in the fire service. I started to write some old memories for friends to read. I wrote these stories so the lay public could understand what was being said: changing jargon, simplifying, and explaining things in more detail.

I called them my "war stories." Well, I must have done something right because people loved to read them. Some told me that they looked forward to the next one. It was frequently suggested that I should collect these war stories together and publish them as a book. I was getting this positive feedback not only from those in the fire service, like old fire buddies and former students that I had taught in recruit school, but also from many friends from the lay public...regular people!

I thought back over my long career and pulled together a variety of stories that stand out in my memory. Some are funny, some are sad, and some make you just stop and think. In the interest of privacy, I removed and/or changed the names of people and places. Readers who might not be familiar with the jargon can refer to the glossary in the back. These stories are written for fun and are not meant to make anyone look or feel foolish. Although these events happened to me in a suburban town, they could have happened anywhere and to anybody. The result of my work is what you now hold in your hand.

Read, and I hope you enjoy!

The Stories

Doing It Right

In the late 80s, I separated from my wife and moved in with Mom for a while. Turned out to be about a year, but then I had to get out before we drove each other crazy. I was fortunate enough to find a room to rent close to work and my kids. It had kind of a parlor and another room for a bedroom. In that bedroom was a fireplace. I asked my landlord and was told that the fireplace was usable. I did a lot of drinking, working, and trying to make enough money to meet the new expenses. I didn't have time to do the little things, like take the trash out, so the fireplace was great. I threw all my burnable trash in there, and when there was enough, I'd burn it all up. Sometimes I'd get some wood and have a nice fire in the evening.

One night, for one reason or another, I had a paper bag filled with some magazines, newspapers, and sheets of paper. Not thinking, I put it in the fireplace and lit the bag. Now, not only was I in the business of putting fires out, but I was paid to work in live fires at the firefighting academy. I was familiar with fire behavior, but this day I wasn't paying attention. Before I knew what happened, the paper bag had burned away, letting all that paper slide out and toward the open front of the fireplace and the small hearth. The paper started to burn bigger, and in a millisecond, the flames were licking the mantle and the paint was darkening. There was no time for thought. The wall would be going in another few seconds.

I didn't have time to get to the kitchen for water; the room would be burning before I got back. Fire spread can be awesome to see, and I knew I had no time. All I had on hand was a plastic, one quart canteen that I kept for late night thirst, but it was probably only about two thirds full. It was go for broke time. I took the cap off and started to sprinkle the water through my fingers over the fire and tried to spread it around and knock down the fire. Sure enough, the fire darkened and the flames died down and I was free to get any embers left with my foot.

Just like I always told recruits at the academy, you don't need much water to put out a fire...if it is used properly. I knocked it down and stopped the spread and put it out with less than a quart of water. I cleaned and repainted the woodwork and the mantle, and thanked Lady Luck for a clear head and knowing how to use water efficiently.

Put on Those Eggs and Hammie, Mammie!

Many moons ago when I worked in the tree business, we were coming home from work one day and I was riding with my friend. We were near the highway and we could see cars parked along the side of the road. A crowd of people was standing on the overpass staring down onto the turnpike.

Well, we stopped to see what was up. I got to the rail and saw a semi on its side with the front half of the trailer still attached. Looking back east, we could see the back half of the trailer. There were probably 150 yards between the two halves. Strewn out in kind of a straight line, were hams. That's right. It was a Colonial meat truck. I don't know just what happened, but there were big smoked shoulders all over the side of the Pike.

The fun began when we saw people walking down the hill and jumping the fence to take the hams. No police had shown up yet. As soon as they did, they tried to stop the thefts, but they couldn't be everywhere at once, so a guy would jump the fence and toss two or three to a friend. Then he'd jump back and they'd run up the hill and disappear with the police yelling at them! It was hilarious to watch—and seeing hams all over the Mass Pike was kind of a treat in itself.

That night and the next day, the news reported that those hams were bad and on their way to be destroyed. That didn't fool anyone, so they stopped saying that after a day or two. I guess they just wrote off their losses.

Some Brush Fires

It's a long time ago and I don't remember some of the details, but one summer day there was a big brush fire up in the north end of town. It was big enough to have the duty officer strike the box for more help. I reported to the fire station and soon was in the passenger seat of an engine responding to the brush fire. The guy driving was a young guy, like me, and had come on the job the same year as me. We were young and full of juice and wanted to get to the fire, so we were moving fast. As we approached the road that we had to turn onto, the driver was going too fast to make the turn. I should have said something, but I didn't.

We came up to the street fast, and I said, "That's where we turn."

The driver looked and stomped on the brakes. All wheels stopped turning as the truck came to a dead stop. The driver put it in reverse, backed up fast, and turned. I never would have believed that an engine could stop that fast, but we both laughed about that for years.

We came to the brush fire in a big grassy field with a big barn in the middle of it. The fire was moving away from me, and we couldn't get any closer with the engine. I grabbed the pre-connected forestry hose from the top of the engine and took off running through the high grass to where the fire was. The hose was three hundred feet long and I had the nozzle in my hand as I ran. It wasn't too bad—until the pump operator filled my hose with water. Suddenly, it got heavy and it almost knocked me off balance. As if that wasn't bad enough, I was still a little short of the fire. The distance between me and the fire meant that I was too far away to be effective putting it out.

I cursed, and then cursed again as the wind shifted and now the fire was blowing toward me. With the wind behind it, there was no way in hell I was going to outrun the fire. I stood there with the nozzle open, throwing as much water as possible on the grass so it wouldn't burn me up when the fire got to me.

We were scared the barn might burn, but we had enough people there to contain the fire before it got to it. Things all ended well. The fire was put out. I never got another brush fire call at that field and I'm surprised. Maybe we were just lucky.

Another brush fire gone awry involved one of our own. The state allows open burning of brush and garden debris from January fifteenth through May first of each year. Residents have to call for permission to burn. Their name and address is taken down, in case we have any problems, and we issue them a burn permit.

Well, we had a firefighter who was off duty and he decided to burn some brush. This guy isn't the brightest light in the forest and doesn't look at the big picture often. His house was next to a busy interstate highway. He lit his fire and things went well. Then it was time for lunch. Being someone who is concerned with his own comfort first, he went inside to eat, leaving the fire unattended. He probably looked at things and decided it would be safe. Well, I guess he heard on his scanner that the duty companies were responding to a brush fire in his neighborhood. He got up and went outside to find that his permit fire had crossed his yard and was now crossing the interstate.

Help came in and the fire was put out, but the fire business has a long memory and ball busting is an art form. When one of our own does something dumb, they're never allowed to forget it.

There was also a guy I knew from the academy who was a captain on a department to our south a ways. This guy drew a burn permit one day. I don't know all the particulars, but in the course of his brush burning, his barn caught fire and burned to the ground. Each year at the academy, they would designate a day as the "Annual Barn Burning" day. The big difference between the two is how the people involved took the ball busting. The guy on my department doesn't take criticism well and gets mad or sulky, while the other guy knew he screwed up and just laughed along with everyone else.

Rising from the Dead

Near the house where I grew up, there stood a big Victorian house. It was at the intersection of two main streets. I remember a front lawn and a hedge lining a sort of crescent shaped driveway. There were big steps leading to a big porch on the front of the house. Each year, the man of the house, an older man who had grown up right there, I'm told, would put on a Santa suit and come out onto the porch roof and wave and throw candy for neighborhood kids. The guy was just the right build, short and kind of stocky, and he did a great job with the kids.

However, it seems there were other forces at work one year. Our Santa had another passion: he liked to drink...alcohol...a lot. One year, he had a few before he came out as Santa, and the next thing you know, he managed to fall off of the roof in front of the neighborhood kids. There was a lot of gasping, laughing, and a great sadness as many believed they had witnessed the demise of Santa.

But this goes deeper. This house was on a big piece of property. The guy was older and out of shape, so he took care of some of it, but left the rest to grow over. There was also a little used shed in the overgrowth. Part of the grown-over part abutted a big, local ballpark. The kids from the local grammar school would cross the street in nice weather and have recess in that park.

One day, long ago, when I myself was one of those kids recessing in the park, word spread like wildfire that someone had found a dead body in the "woods" next to the park. Well, being curious, there was a stampede toward that spot. Sure enough, there it was: the body of a man–older, short, and bald–lying motionless on the ground at the entrance to the shed. Before the recess teachers got the chance to stop anybody (it happened *that* fast), there was a big herd of grade school kids in kind of a semicircle around the dead man.

We heard a door open and looked at the house. A small, older lady had just come out and started in our direction. The crowd parted as she passed through. She bent over the body and whispered and pushed and shook it for a couple of minutes. Then, before our very eyes, the dead man sat up. The Mrs. helped him to his feet. After that, she yelled at all of us for being there and they started for the house. Then the teachers arrived, and just like *that*...it was over.

Or, so it seemed.

But wait! What if one of the school kids was sharp enough to see the similarities between the dead man and Santa? Word could have spread. We all could have experienced a premature abandonment of that childhood Santa thing. Our lives *could* have been destroyed.

Confined Space

There are more things that a firefighter does other than putting out fires. There are medical calls and technical rescue, to name two. Tech rescue encompasses rope rescue, trench rescue, and confined space rescue. A team could be working all of these types of calls all at once in one incident. Though rope rescue and confined space rescue are taught at the academy in recruit training, I've often felt that they're only teaching enough to get someone killed. If it were up to me, time would be better spent practicing working with ladders or doing more live fire training. I've always thought that the tech rescue training should be done after basic training for those who wish to become tech rescue technicians. Those guys belong to regional teams that train at least once a month on specialized rescue techniques. That way they keep sharp. You can't take a class once and think you know everything.

Some large towns or cities may have their own in-house tech rescue teams. Near me, there are regional teams that can be called in to help in an incident, if needed. I once looked into trying to get a space on a local team for my fire department, but the chief wasn't on board with that idea. He never said exactly why, but I suspect that it was a money issue. It was always a money issue with that chief.

He was a wheeler and dealer and we never knew what the hell he was doing. He knew people and he was always trying to get his friends into our department's training. They showed up at a live burn which ended up being full of his buddies from some arson squad or another. The burns were all geared towards the arson squad, but we lit them and put them out until the arson people were done and the drill was over. Then they left, along with our chief, leaving us to clean up the mess. We were there until after dark picking up shit. He was more preoccupied with his buddies than his department's training.

His pals sometimes returned favors, too. One day, the boss came out of his office and said that he got room to get six people in a confined space rescue program put on by the state water authority. I got one of the slots. A couple of days later, (we never had much notice from our chief), and we were meeting at the water resources yard in a city east of us. We took our own cars to get there. It didn't take long to realize that this was a program designed for and geared towards the employees of the water authority.

We used the tools and practiced getting victims out of tunnels. It was interesting and fun to take part in, but it was not the type of confined space training that firefighters need. Afterwards, there wasn't much talk about the class we had attended. The boss never asked me how it went.

A few weeks went by and one day the chief asked me who was with me when we took that confined space rescue class. I told him and he repeated the names and said something about us "having the training." I wasn't sure what he meant. After all, he couldn't expect us to do confined space work, could he? We weren't trained. We had only taken one class, and not even one designed for firefighters.

Not too long after that, we took delivery of a tripod and a bunch of other tech rescue tools. Then the chief issued each firefighter on our department a confined space rescue helmet.

I told this tale to a friend at the academy. Then I said to him, "We don't *do* confined space rescues." He broke into laughter. My chief's reputation was well-known!

My confined space helmet sits on a shelf behind me as I write this. My son once used it to go cave exploring. Other than that, the kids played with it until I took it and put it with other memorabilia. Another guy on the department gave his to his son for a bicycle helmet. I couldn't say what happened to the rest.

But the boss wasn't done yet. Shortly after I became the training officer, the chief instructed me to buy enough rope to issue each firefighter an eight-foot piece of rope to carry with them. Now I think a piece of rope is always handy to have and I do keep one, but I was sure that anyone who would use a rope had already gotten one. The rest wouldn't ever use them, but I did as I was ordered and got the rope. They were issued and the questions like, "What the hell do I need that for?" came, as well as some jokes and laughter. My rope right now is made into a monkey's fist, as are two other ropes that had been discarded. That's a hard knot to master and they look good.

Then the boss got the idea that rope bags would be nice for all the firefighters to have. It was never clear just what the rope was to be used for—bail outs or wide area search or whatever. There was never any talk about training or anything. I guess he figured that we'd hold on to the rope and gravity would do the rest.

I had to go buy a box of flag hooks and carabineers. The boss picked up some empty personal rope bags. Then he came up with a whole bunch of Kevlar rope. I was told to put 50 feet of rope in each bag with a flag hook on one end and a carabineer on the other. Hell, I could hardly even cut the stuff! Those were a pain in the ass to make and it was all a big joke anyway.

Characteristically, the chief lost interest in the project, so the rope bags sat in a storage closet until I retired. Then, half a dozen bags found their way into the stuff I was bringing home from the fire station. Nobody ever missed them...and we *still* didn't do confined space rescue!

The Night New York Was Closed

For years, from when we became a couple until the kids were in school, we went to Manhattan for Thanksgiving. My wife is from New York City. It was a great deal of fun seeing the Macy's parade from Times Square. Then my wife's family would have a gathering at her parent's apartment. Not coming from a family that did that, it was a great time for me as I really liked her family. We would go uptown the night before and watch the balloons for the parade being inflated. Plus, the city is beautiful during the holidays.

Well, one year, before we had any kids, an aunt was ill and couldn't be there on Thursday, Thanksgiving. So it was decided to postpone the special dinner for two days until Saturday so everyone could be there.

Thanksgiving finally came and my wife and I did our usual things, like see the parade and sightsee. We spent the day out and about and looked around.

The evening came and we went back to the apartment and found it was pot luck for dinner. There was nothing in the fridge that put lead in the old pencil, so we went out to get some food. It was as deserted as I've ever seen the city. We walked all around and couldn't find anything open. I never would have believed it happening in New York...the "city that never sleeps." Well, if they weren't sleeping, they must have left town for the night. There was nothing open, not even those places that are open 24 hours, 365 days a year. I often wondered why they had locks on their doors. Now I know. The nearest we came to food was an avenue over in the West Village, where FDNY Ladder 6 was parked and the crew was handing out meals to the homeless. No, I didn't get in line!

A tenacious search eventually produced a small ice cream shop that was open. It wasn't much of a dinner. We made up for that two days later. But I have never seen the city so quiet and deserted. Bless those guys from Ladder 6.

Test of Time

Many years ago, one of the many side jobs I had on my days off from the fire department was house painting. One day, I was working at a house that was right across the street from the captain I worked for at that time. The captain was friends with the residents of that house. I met the lady of the house while I was painting and we had a few moments to talk. I told her my name and what I did for a living.

A couple of years later, those people had moved to Pennsylvania somewhere. The captain came up to me one day at the firehouse and told me he had gotten a call from those old neighbors of his. It seems that the lady I had met while painting her house was in church in Pennsylvania with her husband. While listening to the minister's sermon–I'm not really sure what the topic could have been–the minister said something like, "When I was a kid, I had a friend named Lewie LeBlanc. I used to have a lot of fun with Lewie. I don't know where he is now..."

Well, that lady in the congregation knew very well where Lewie LeBlanc was and what became of him! She told the minister and she called her old neighbors so the captain could tell me. It all kind of ended there...or so I thought.

Some years after that, it was winter–my birthday, in fact. We weren't doing much that afternoon when the phone rang. I was in the attic and my wife answered. She brought the phone to me and told me who it was—no one she knew, but I sure knew him. It was that minister! I had known him for most of my life and was always friendly with him. I was overjoyed to hear from him. He contacted me because he remembered my birthday and thought he'd call. It was incredible to hear from him again, but sadly he told me that he had just been diagnosed with cancer. He did go on Facebook briefly, but as he got sicker, he dropped out. It's an honor that someone remembered me that fondly after all the years since we'd last seen each other. You never really know how you might have affected someone else's life, or if you're ever really remembered by the people you meet through life.

He did pass on a few years ago, another victim of cancer. Rest in peace! I guess good friendship will last through the ages.

Loose Moose

I read a post on Facebook where someone mentioned Mutual of Omaha's Wild Kingdom. Remember that? It used to be on TV on Sundays. As kids, we watched as Marlin Perkins would anesthetize rhinos and bears and the like, and move them hundreds of miles to an area where they were safe and couldn't get into trouble.

I remember the time, about 25 or 30 years ago, when a young moose showed up near the town center. The local authorities were at a complete loss as to what to do, sooooo they waited until there were three major network news teams on scene covering the story live. Then they got a man with a rifle and blew the moose away on national television on the prime time news. They claimed that they had nothing else they could do. Old Marlin Perkins must have been busy that day...no doubt they called him.

Irony

In the early 70s, I worked in the neighboring town for the highway department. It was a good job. Working for two years there, I got to know all the town workers: police, fire, school, etc. I even got on the call fire department in that town as well as my own. That way I could go to their drills for more training. Yea, maybe I'm a geek, but I liked what I did.

The center of town is an interesting place. It's very busy with all the old townies and some new ones gathering at the coffee shop in the morning. I met a man there who was on the fire department, sort of. You see, at that time, the town had an unusual position that they called "temporary firefighter," and that's what the badge said. The guy was a townie. He was, I believe, part of an old family that was into real estate. This guy was on the call department, but whenever he wanted to work full-time, he'd go to the fire chief and get assigned to a group for a while. That was very unusual then and unheard of now.

I got along well with this guy and saw him often in the town center, sometimes working at the fire department or just stopping for coffee. He was around my age, maybe a year or two older, and he seemed to be active and in fair shape. I used to see him at the gym nights when I went to work out.

After a couple of years, my own appointment to the fire department in my town came up and I didn't see that guy too often–sometimes on calls if he was "on duty." After a while, I went to work at the fire academy part-time. In my first book, War Stories: Some Memories from the Firehouse Years, he is mentioned. He is in the story about doing CPR and having the ambulance stop short. I sailed through the doorway and into the cab and never touched the walls! My friend was the ambulance driver.

After a while, the town decided to abolish the position of temporary firefighter and make it a full-time, permanent position. It was offered to my friend and he accepted. He came to the academy for training and I saw him there, but some time into the program, it was found that the guy was on a cardiac medication and told no one about it. Grounds for dismissal...and he was, and so I lost contact with him for many years.

One morning, a couple of years ago, I found out that the town had had a house fire in which the resident died. A day or so later, I got the name of the victim. It was my friend. He was the only one in the house and it seems that he couldn't get out. It's hard for me to think that anyone with firefighter training couldn't have gotten out of the house. I do think that smoke detectors were up and working. But, you have to ask, if they were not in place...why not? This was a resident with at least some basic knowledge of what to do in a fire and how to get out.

That whole story, as I know it, is just bizarre when thinking about what happened and the person involved.

Some Winter Memories

I remember, as I grew up, watching my mother hanging out the wash. A big wooden basket, like a big apple basket, would be sitting on the ground full of clean clothes, and a bag of clothespins would be hanging on the line. We never had a dryer, so all year round she had to hang the wash outside. It would be absolute chaos when a line broke when loaded with wet, clean clothes. As soon as I got tall enough to reach, it was my job to get out and replace the line and kind of dust off the clothes. In the winter, it was my job to shovel the driveway–yes, shovel, no snow blower–and a few other paths, including one to the clothes line and all around it, so Mom could work there.

Winter was tough. When the temp went down, the clothes didn't dry. None of us had an extensive wardrobe. We had enough clothing to cover our backsides and then some, but not an awful lot. Sooooo, it was common to have immediate need for something on the line. Wet was bad enough, but from November through most of March, the clothes were frozen stiff.

We had an old oil furnace and steam radiators throughout the house. Those things might have looked like hell, but they sure threw some heat. Many a winter day we would come in with frozen hands and feet. We would lie on the floor and put our stockinged feet right on the radiator and warm up. We would put wet gloves and mittens on the radiators to dry, and so...that's where the laundry went...well, at least the things that were most needed right away. The rest kind of got hung where there was room. I remember taking dungarees–yes, we called them that, not jeans–I'd take them off the radiator and put them on and...ooohhhh, they were sooooo warm!

We also had kind of a strange kitchen stove. I remember getting it when I was little. It was a normal stove on one end, and the other end was an oil-fired heater. We would put these special five gallon metal oil cans full of range oil into–well, something like a Poland Springs water cooler–and the oil would feed the heater in the left end of the stove. We would refill those cans down in the cellar where we had two 55-gallon barrels with a spigot on each.

When we called for an oil delivery, we had to specify whether we wanted range oil or fuel oil. The fuel oil was for the furnace and was filled from the outside. For the range oil, the delivery man would bring the hose right into the cellar and fill the barrels. It was all legal then, but it sure wouldn't fly nowadays! We used that heater part of the stove until it got destroyed one summer during a thunderstorm when the house was struck by lightning. But, that's another story...just another memory.

Bad Timing

My wife and I bought our house in 1997 from my aunt who had owned it since the early 60s. I have a kind of large family and until the 80s, most lived pretty close by. Each year, the family had a cookout. Sure, some were at other relatives' homes, but by far, the majority were at this house.

It all started as a family party. There were always a few close friends, but mostly family. As the years went by, the family spread out and went their own ways, but that cookout stayed on and became an annual party that my uncle and aunt threw for their friends and family. It was never unusual to find someone there that you didn't know; someone there knew them!

They had a small pool then. It was about 12 feet, round, and wonderful in the July heat while running around with my cousins. No matter how full that pool got, it was still wet and fun!

When a bunch of guys get together with horseshoe games and a cookout in July–factor in all the beer that got consumed–it was only inevitable that someone was going to get thrown into the pool. It often turned into a frenzy. No one was safe. You'd be targeted by the mob and you were chased down until they caught you, and into the pool you went. People who came to the cookouts every year could see when the writing was on the wall and either took part or hid.

Well, at the cookout one year, the weather was nice and hot and the beer flowed like water. After a short time spent swilling beer, the boys were getting frisky. It wasn't too long before someone was grabbed and into the pool they went. That was all the provocation they needed. The mob formed and fed on itself.

Someone just got thrown in when someone else looked up and saw a man walking across the backyard. They didn't know him, and the poor guy was dressed nice...neat and casual. Well, none of that ever made any difference before. The mob turned, and with a collective war cry, they set upon the man. He knew enough not to struggle too much; it wouldn't do him any good. He must have been reasonably sure that he wasn't going to be killed, but he didn't fight it as he was picked up bodily by that howling mob, carried across the yard, and unceremoniously dumped into the pool, to the howls and laughter of all the participants. The guy got out and disappeared and was quickly for-forgotten about...until later.

Someone who had talked to him found out that he was from out of town and was going somewhere. He was lost, and seeing all those people in the backyard, he stopped for directions. He left his wife in the car and walked into the hornets' nest, such was the backyard.

After hearing this new information, there were a lot of "holy shits" and a lot of laughter. The guy must have had quite a sense of humor. I don't think I could have reacted like he did. I wonder if he ever got his directions.

Big Bad John

Each Valentine's Day I'm reminded of another story along my life's path. The connection to Valentine's Day may seem small, but I think it was very significant at that time.

I had a cousin named John. He was a couple of years older than me. He was lean and wiry, even as a kid. He was very strong and muscular. He was also kind of a bully. He was tough and could handle himself without any fear in any altercation.

I was the kind of kid who avoided fights. I did fight, but only when I was blind with fury. I was afraid of John, and he used to take any opportunity to pick on me. I don't think he would have hurt me, but I didn't know that at the time. I avoided him like the plague, and I said often that I hated him. We certainly never hung out together!

Well, the years passed and John graduated from high school and went into the army. There was a draft, but he enlisted. He wanted to learn diesel mechanics. He went away and I didn't see him again for many years. I heard that he did learn diesel mechanics, but when he received his orders for Vietnam, he opted for and got into ranger training. Figured if he was gonna go, he might as well fight. And fight he did. He had many souvenirs that he brought back and stories to tell.

I didn't keep in touch. I heard that he had gotten out of the army and was living in Kansas with his wife, who he had met out there, I guess. I got on the fire department and got married and lived in the old family homestead. My grandparents lived nearby and I used to visit them often.

One summer, an uncle of mine, a real wild man, got on his motorcycle and rode it from Florida to Massachusetts and stayed with his parents. He wasn't really that much older than me, and I always liked him, so I started to spend some time with him.

One day, my uncle said, "Let's go visit John."

Apparently, he was now living nearby. I didn't know John was around, but said, "OK," and we went to a house that John's family owned where he was staying. I wasn't too sure how things would turn out, but as it was, things went well. We had both grown up–no more bully and his victim. My uncle and I started to spend a lot of time with John. His marriage was on the rocks and ended when his wife moved back to Kansas. I spent lots of time with John, even after our uncle hopped on his bike and rode back to Florida. But it was very casual and just small talk.

Then one night in the wee hours, the phone rang. It was my aunt telling me that my grandmother had died that night. Of all her grandchildren, they called only me because I was always visiting her. I was supposed to visit earlier that day, but couldn't make it, so I called and said I'd stop by in a day or two. Nana spent the day baking cookies, went to bed that night, and had a heart attack and died...It was Valentine's Day.

In the aftermath of the family gatherings and the funeral, I spent lots of time with John. I think it was then that we became fast friends. During that time, I met John's girlfriend. She was very pregnant and was living with John. I visited them often, even after the baby was born. It was great having a friend like him. It seemed that there was nothing he couldn't do and you always felt safe when with him. Yes, John was still a badass, but he gave me a respect that said he was my friend. He liked to drink and was a real wild man, but I loved hanging with him.

When he told me that he and his girl were getting married, I asked if I was invited to the wedding. He replied by telling me that I was going to be his best man! I was honored. No one had ever asked me to do that before, and I wasn't asked...I was told! I felt great about it and still do.

He and his girl had a very volatile relationship. The wedding never took place, but they had a second child together.

There was one time when he and I were out drinking more that we should. I was tipsy, and it seemed that he was, too. We got up and headed for the stairs to leave the bar. As soon as he hit the bottom step, my cousin went down. I bent over and couldn't feel a pulse. I had had a bit to drink, but my mind seemed clear. I gave him a couple of breaths and compressed his chest a couple of times. He came to, but wasn't coherent. An ambulance was called and I rode with him. He fared well and a couple of years later when we were talking, he told me that I had saved his life. I never really thought about it, but maybe I did.

Well, time passed and life got in the way of our travels. We stayed in touch, but other things needed to be done. A few years down the road, the phone rang in the early morning hours. It was an uncle of mine telling me that John had been killed in a traffic accident on his motorcycle. He was a good rider, but wild. He came up on a stop sign, one dark October night, going too fast. He managed to lay the bike down, but when he got off, a car hit him killing him...another family funeral. That was the last time I ever shed tears.

We had been enemies for so many years, but we got together and were best friends at the time John died. It seems ironic now, but that's the way it happened, and I'm happy to have known him and gotten close to him for even a short time.

John's brother now owns the house where John lived then. It's right on Main Street. For years, the family would gather there to watch the July 4th parade as it passed in front of the house. It was nice to see the cousins and others that I didn't see often. One year, during the parade, one of them took me aside and pointed to a young man standing in the doorway of the house. I was asked who that guy looked like. It took a minute or so, but as the young man turned, I saw my cousin John standing there. They told me that it was John's son. He was the spitting image! The little boy that I had last seen at his father's funeral was there before me, and looking just like the man I remembered.

We talked a bit and I was pointed toward a young lady sitting near the street. It was John's daughter, the same little girl I held as a baby. We talked and I was told that their mother had died of cancer a few years before. I'm so very thankful that I had another chance with John, my cousin, my friend...and it started on Valentine's Day. This was a treat I never expected. I lost a grandmother, but gained a lifelong friend. Rest in peace, John.

Someday

As one of the "older" guys on the fire department and at the state fire academy, I often heard remarks about being old and feeble, how ancient I was and the like. All in good fun, of course–at least most of it! I often answered this with, "Enjoy yourselves at my expense, if you want. But remember that someday, some young prick who isn't even born yet will do the same to you!"

And that's the truth!

What If I Had Listened?

I remember when I was playing Pop Warner football my last year. We had all new coaches. The old ones had sons who were either too big or too old to play anymore. I got to know one of the coaches pretty well, and actually got to know his wife and his four grammar school-age daughters. They were nice people. They also had a son who was alright, I guess. Trouble was, he kept hanging around with older kids and trying to impress them to fit in. It was the same when we all got to high school. You could see him at all the parties trying to be one of the guys. I kind of stayed away from him. I guess I just got sick of listening to him. Stand back and you could see that he was kind of a whipping boy for the group he was trying to belong to.

One late spring night at a party, the kid must have gotten mouthy again because someone punched him in the stomach–hard–and he was on the ground, gasping hard. It was the kind of thing one would have expected from a recipient of such a punch, but this was really bad. Plus, I knew that the guy had asthma. I don't know who the hell else knew, but this was getting bad. Next thing I knew, there were about five other guys trying to carry a now semi-conscious boy toward the house. They had trouble holding him, and he dropped on the ground a couple of times. I walked over and looked at him. The kid looked bad. I sent someone in the house to call the fire department for an ambulance. Funny how when others panic, if you sound like you know what you're doing, people do what you say. We had no idea what to do for him.

Then the kid I sent to the house came back and said that the parents of the kid throwing the party talked to their son and he told them things were alright, so no ambulance was called. The guy told me that and I got up and marched into the house and demanded a telephone. The lady and man of the house just pointed to a wall phone. No 911 at that time, so I looked up the number and reported the problem to the fire department.

The dispatcher yelled, "What the hell is the address?"

I didn't know the address, but told him there was a big party and they couldn't miss the place.

He really got agitated with me, so I turned and barked at the parents asking for the house number. Then we hung up, and I walked out like it was my own house. Outside, I just blended in with the others at the party and watched when the ambulance came and took him away.

The kid recovered OK, and maybe it wasn't as bad as it looked, but it looked very bad. I've lost track of those people now, but I wonder what would have happened if I listened and didn't worry about it. What if I had listened?

Halloween Memory

Halloween has changed a lot over the years. I think more attention is being paid to the safety of the kids, young and old. Many schools have a place where the teens can hang out and stay safe. My school always held a Halloween dance. Those were often pretty wild, but I guess being there and not driving around probably did save some lives. Of course, there are always the crazies that are going to get into trouble anyway, and that kept that night kind of a busy one for the fire department.

That high school dance was still being held when I was a new guy on the job. One year, we got a call to respond to the high school for some kind of injury at the Halloween dance. I was on the ambulance, and when we arrived, the south side engine was just getting there also. There were teens in costume everywhere. The dance was well attended, but we found our patient without any trouble. It was a girl, dressed as an Indian, on the floor crying and holding a badly dislocated knee. She was on a table dancing when the table collapsed, and she was in a lot of pain.

Well, she latched onto my hand and held on tight. The knee was immobilized and she was placed on the stretcher and rolled out to the ambulance and driven to the hospital, all the while holding my hand. She didn't let go until the staff at the ER started to do what needed to be done. Then she let go and we left.

Some years later, I worked as a part-time maintenance mechanic at a swimming pool near the high school. The duties were light because they didn't have any money to fix things, so I puttered around and did some minor chores and checked on the pool chemicals. I got to know some of the lifeguards, who were mostly teens, and more often than not, they were girls– and probably still are. Sometimes I'd stop to talk and ask the guards if they had any reports of broken stuff, not that I would be given the go-ahead to fix anything.

One day, I was finishing up checking things at the pool and I was getting ready to leave when I went to check with the guard. It was a young lady who I hadn't seen before, so I introduced myself. We talked a few minutes and I noticed that her knee had had some injury. It looked like a roadmap with lines going everywhere. There were a couple of big scars on it. Well, being me, I asked what had happened to her knee. She answered that she had hurt it in a fall, if I remember correctly. Then memories came flooding back and I knew who she was. I started talking.

"At the Halloween dance...you were dressed like an Indian... and a table collapsed with you standing on it..."

She looked at me with an astonished expression on her face. She asked if I was there, and I answered her by telling her that I had held her hand all the way to the hospital. There was no real recognition. She remembered the hand, but not really anything else. I got up to leave and told her I was glad her knee was working again. I don't think she ever expected to hear how well I remembered. That's just the way I am.

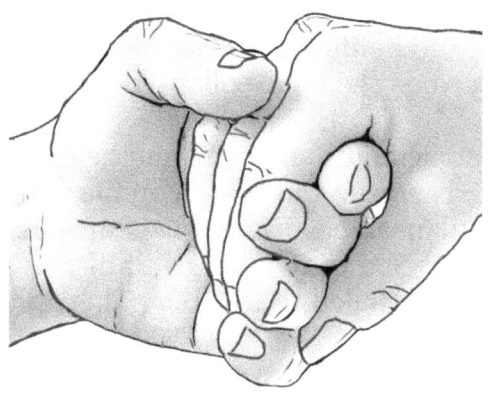

Oh Boy...

There have been many times when I was in someone's home and saw something that the family didn't mean to leave around, be it money, pictures, valuables, or just about anything else. I don't really know if they wished that we hadn't seen things, or if they really didn't care. We never said anything, except among ourselves.

One summer evening, we got a call for the ambulance to transport a woman with some sort of altered mental status. I arrived with the south side engine and we were already inside when the ambulance got there. The patient was a middle-aged lady in a very agitated state. She was yelling and wouldn't talk to us. She was making no sense, and when we got her on the stretcher, she would not lie still. I thought that she could injure herself or one of us. We had been told that there was a section 12, an involuntary committal paper, waiting at the hospital. That meant that we had to take her. With no cooperation from her, I ordered four-point restraints. This means we tie wrists and ankles to the stretcher. I always hated to do that, but sometimes it had to be done. We loaded the stretcher into the ambulance, and she was off to the hospital.

Then we were told by police that neighbors reported that our patient had had a pretty intense fight with her teenage son, and no one knew where the boy was. So, we and the police had to search the house. Now, this lady was no housekeeper; there was junk everywhere. In all fairness, some of the mess could have happened during the fight, but not all.

I went into the bedroom. The blankets and sheets had been pulled off of the bed and were part of the mess that was the bedroom. I stepped down on something and looked down. I saw a dildo on the floor under my feet. I just chuckled a bit. The lady would probably be mortified if she knew what I had found.

Then the captain came in the room. He walked toward me and I told him to be careful not to trip as I pointed down. He laughed a bit and went out. Finding no sign of the son, I went outside. I passed the captain and a police officer going toward the bedroom for a look at the recent find. We were dismissed and went back to the firehouse.

A short time later, I started to hear my chops being busted. The captain had told everyone that I had been laughing and making sure I showed the toy to everybody. I only showed it to the captain and kept quiet, but no one believed that!

Well…I guess I deserved it. That's exactly the kind of thing I would do. The firehouse can be a tough place, if you have a thin skin.

No Gazelles

When my kids were small, the family bought a small cottage near the beach. It had a fireplace going into a brick chimney, but we thought it best not to use it. Instead, we built a shelving unit that slid right into the firebox, taking up the whole opening for the fireplace. We just had to close off the top of the chimney until we could get it taken down.

The chimney had one of those wire screen toppers. My young daughter asked what it was for. We explained that it was to keep animals from getting in. She replied, "Like gazelles?" Yes, like gazelles. We still laugh over that.

Thinking about what she said makes me think of all the different things I've seen in chimneys over the years. Now, I'm not sure that the firefighters from bigger, busier places even do calls like we get, but in the smaller suburban fire departments, we get calls for everything. People call and say that their homes "smell funny," or "something just isn't right," or "I think there's something in my chimney."

Sometimes we'd get the dreaded call when someone said they wanted to build a fire so they opened the flue and a bird or a bat flew out, or maybe even a raccoon or squirrel fell out and now they're loose in the house. We had to respond to all these calls. We'd have to deal with the problem, whatever it was, before we could leave. That usually meant that we had to try to capture whatever beast had invaded their home. We didn't have anybody else we could call to come take care of it, so it was up to us.

We've chased birds through houses trying to corral the thing in one room so we could work out some plan to capture it without hurting it. I remember a couple of times when we were able to chase a bird right out an open window or door, but that was rarely the case. We used bags, baskets, or maybe a light blanket to capture the poor thing and we'd release it outside. I have chased squirrels, chipmunks, and even mice, trying to herd them into a box to take them outside.

Some of the best animal calls were the bats flying around the house. People have an aversion to bats, it seems. They open the fireplace flue and a bat flies out. Sometimes they fly out when someone opens an attic door, too. You haven't seen a shit show until you've seen a call like that. We'd try to corral it, but it would turn and dive and everyone would run. Each time we'd put up some kind of net to catch it, the bat would dart around it. After a while, we could usually pin it between a net and the wall and take it outside with a heavily gloved hand.

I remember answering a call one time because a snake slithered out of a fireplace and disappeared in the lady's house. We never found it, in spite of a thorough search. The lady of the house wasn't pleased, but what can you do? I guess we could have pretended we had gotten it and she would have never known the difference, but it didn't occur to anyone.

We always had to be extra careful not to harm the animal when trying to catch it. No matter how appalled or scared the family is, they would have complained loudly if any harm had come to it. Yes, even with us being careful, we did have times when the animal might have gotten injured, but ran away when we got it outside.

So, my darling daughter…there are many animals that could get into the chimney and I guess gazelles can too…I guess.

Birthday Tours

It is a tradition in the fire department that the jobs that no one really wants to do are always the responsibility of the new guy. Of course, everyone gets their share of the daily duties, but when extra things crop up, the new guy gets them. They have to do things like wash the chief's car or wedge shut an open sprinkler head with that cold water pouring down on top of them. The new guy also gets to guide station tours for a family or a bunch of school kids, and though we didn't allow the cake and gifts part of birthday parties at the firehouse, station tours for groups of kids at a birthday party were common.

I was the new guy for a bunch of years, so I got pretty good at it. I discovered early that kids don't care where the water goes in or comes out. They just want to sit in the engine and play with the gear. Even the parents or teachers are interested, to a point. None of them have any idea how we perform our trade, so simplicity is a must, even with the grownups. I even had a station tour for my own son's birthday one year. I did that one on a day when I was off duty, so I could have food and cake, too. Often, a few days after a tour, I would get a big envelope with my name on it containing a bunch of thank you letters from the kids themselves.

A while ago, I got a letter that was written to me by the parents of a little boy. They had arranged to bring their son and a few friends to the firehouse for the boy's fifth birthday—no cake, just the guided tour. But this day, it was different.

It was quiet, so after I gave the usual talk about what they should do if the bell goes off while they were visiting, I took out my gear and put it on, along with an airpack. I showed the kids how fast we get dressed and how all that gear protects us. They were thrilled, and so were the parents.

Then the very next thing was just luck. We had taken delivery of a brand new engine that morning. It didn't even have tools or hose on it yet. If you know how to talk to kids, you can get a lot of mileage out of telling them that they're the very first ones to sit in this engine and pull the horn cord. They could also stand where the hose was going to go. They loved it, and the parents did, too.

Lastly, just as they were getting ready to finish up and were saying their thank yous, we got a call for the ambulance. I don't remember where or what the call was, but we told the kids where to stand to be safely out of our way, and the parents made sure they got there. My partner and I got into the ambulance and left with the lights and siren on. When we got back, they were gone.

A day or two later, when I was on duty, I got a thank you card from the parents. They were full of high praise of going the extra mile and taking the time to make things interesting. They were impressed that we spent so much time with the kids and kept their attention and made their day. They closed their note by saying, "You were marvelous." Good community relations!

> *Thank you*
>
> We are particularly grateful for the long time you spent with us, your kindness and patience with the kids and your thorough demonstration of the trucks and facility. You were marvelous.
>
> We hope it wasn't anything too serious, but your exit really put the icing on the cake."

I Wasn't There

I lived in the old family homestead growing up and for a while after when I bought it from my parents. The house next to mine was a two-family. The owners lived upstairs. They had a son, who was several years older than me, but he and his friends were very good to me, and I got to know them all from early childhood. The downstairs was always rented.

When his parents died, the son inherited the house. It was then that the downstairs was rented to people I knew who were my age. They were a couple that I had known in high school. They used to comment on all the little baby clothes on the clothesline when we had our first child. Before very long, the lady next door was pregnant. I remember when the baby was born and came home. About this time, they were looking for a house to buy. They found one very close by and moved out of my immediate neighborhood.

Not too long after, I was outside in my yard and noticed the fire ambulance moving fast down the street across from the ballpark. I didn't think anything about it until a day or two later. I found out that the ambulance had been heading to that couple's new home for the baby who wasn't breathing. I seem to recall that it was SIDS, but I think there was some question of an allergic reaction to a shot that the baby had just gotten.

Babies and children are some of the hardest calls firefighters do and I have seen a lot of them, but I was just so grateful that they had moved before it happened or I might have been the one that they came running to see first. I was prepared, but I'm just as glad I wasn't there.

Dropping the Eves

Our firehouse was in a crowded building shared with the town hall and the police department. When the town hall moved out, that left us sharing the building with just the police department. We did our best to divide up a building that was never meant to house two public safety departments. When all was done, the police and fire dispatch centers were joined together and manned by civilians. The old police dispatch area was converted to our chief's office and some other space. We got an area they made into a fitness room and the police got the rest. It wasn't a great set up, but it was home. Firefighters make do with what they've got a lot of the time, and make it work.

One thing that didn't get moved was the police cell block. I forget how many cells they had then, maybe two or three, but the cell block was right next to our chief's office and separated by a simple stud and drywall wall. There was usually nothing going on, but when the police locked up some drunk or other ruckus-starting fool, we could hear their antics and yelling from the firehouse–better from the chief's office. We spent a lot of nights and weekends listening to the ravings of one who wants to kill the world, but come morning, he looks much more passive when they take him out for arraignment, hangover and all.

They had a guy–a regular customer. Remember that drunk, Otis, on the Andy Griffith Show? He would come in and lock himself up and sleep it off. There was a guy in our town that sometimes got to drinking and didn't take his meds. He'd come in and they'd lock him up and for several hours we would listen to him rave and yell. We didn't need the chief's office for that. You could hear that guy all over the firehouse.

We heard some pretty entertaining things through the wall in the chief's office. Of course, he did lock the door, but come on...we're firefighters, and locks were made for honest people!

Mountain Memories

I just took a walk outside and sat on my little park bench under the cedar tree in my front yard and toked a bowl. As I looked up through the branches with the water droplets hanging down on this cold wet afternoon, a memory came to me. It was a memory of a day that I count among my best of times. Funny thing is that we didn't do much of anything that day.

Back in the 70s, I used to do a lot of backpacking and camping–not real long trips, but a week to ten days. Because we wanted to stay in the woods, my friend and I would take the bus from a station that used to be near me. We'd ride the bus all the way north to the White Mountains. Then we'd go in on a trail. We always had some kind of plan because we had no car with us and had to come out somewhere near a bus stop to get home. I made this same trip with several different friends over a few years, but I had one guy who was my backpacking buddy and I went with him the most.

There was one time I went with my cousin, if I might stray from the subject a bit. Cous and I went out on a drinking binge the night before. We drank far too much draft beer. We felt crappy in the morning, as you might imagine, but things got better as we rode the bus.

There was a bathroom in the back of the bus. People used it from time to time. Then my cousin stood up to go to the can; he said he had to take a leak. He was in there for a few minutes and a couple of people came and stood waiting for a turn.

Suddenly, this positively raunchy odor filled the back of the bus. A second later, I heard the door unlatch and out came that stench and my cousin in the middle of it all with a nonchalant look on his face. The people who were waiting for their turn returned to their seats and people were craning their necks to look back in our direction. My cousin sat down in his seat like nothing was going on.

I said to him, "I thought you had to take a leak?"
He said that was what he did.
I asked where that smell had come from.
He answered, "I farted."

What could I say?

But back to the subject...My buddy and I spent a whole day just staying ahead of a thunderstorm as we tried to make it up the mountainside to a shelter we knew was on the other side of the peak. We broke the tree line just as the storm hit. We were running over rocks with the storm all around us. We made the shelter.

After staying there for three days in rain and fog, we hiked down to the road and walked a ways. We came to a small campground, and as the weather was still iffy, we got a campsite and set up our two-man mountain tent. Our packs wouldn't fit inside, so we covered them with space blankets right outside the tent, and we packed the small tent with clothes and sleeping bags and crawled in. The next morning, it was pouring rain and it lasted all day, but it was dry in the tent. We spent the day napping and talking and laughing.

I set up a Sterno stove outside under the fly and roasted hot dogs over it on a hunting knife. We ate and snacked and slept and talked all day, then went to sleep for the night. The next day, the sun came out and we were on our way.

That day, rammed in a small tent in the rain, is a memory I'm very fond of. I took many camping trips with this friend until we couldn't anymore. I lost my friend to cancer a few years ago, but his memory is alive with stories like this...so many stories.

We've Come a Long Way, Baby

I remember a time when waiting was almost unbearable for me. It was back in the 80s when AIDS reared its ugly head. No one knew what it was and people were terror-stricken. The terror and lack of knowledge extended to the emergency services as well. A procedure was established to deal with unprotected exposures to blood and body fluids for personnel working on the street, the first responders.

One day, when I was working at station 2, we responded to a vehicle accident a short distance away. My partner and I in engine 2 were first due. We found a pickup truck that had struck a utility pole. There was heavy front-end damage and an unconscious young man was the only person in the vehicle. He was lying on his back on the bench seat.

I took the jump kit and went in the passenger door to examine the patient. Back then, there were no precautions taken and I was above his face. I saw that his mouth was open and was filling with blood from facial injuries. Before I had any chance to react, the young man woke up and coughed forcefully, and all that blood hit me in the face and eyes.

We extricated our victim and got ready to transport him. I told the captain that I was going to report my unprotected exposure at the hospital. When we got there, we took care of our patient, and then I went to the nurse at the desk and told her what had happened. I said I wanted to report an unprotected exposure.

She looked at me like I had two heads. No one had any idea what to do. Remember, this was very long ago and no one at our level of training knew anything about AIDS, much less what to do.

Well, they took my blood pressure and a blood sample. They had me talk to a counselor and sent me home with instructions to use condoms and avoid exposing others to my body fluids. Things could have been simplified if the young man who was our patient would consent to a blood test to see if he was infected, but he wasn't having any of that. I had to go back to that hospital each month for a year for a blood test and a talk with the counselor.

Waiting for the results of my blood tests was agony that stretched out over a year. The protocol in place to deal with an exposure seemed to have gone no further than the administration. The people in the ER had heard a protocol was coming, but it seems that I was the very first one to report an exposure. Everyone was groping around in the dark. No one understood the thing we were concerned with. That waiting was agony. We've come a very long way since then!

Cutting Costs

We were a small fire department of just twenty-four full-time people and a maximum of ten call firefighters, though the call department usually had fewer than ten. The call people didn't work any shifts at all. We had two firehouses in town, both manned. Station 2 was on the south end of town and was staffed by two firefighters. Station 1 was the headquarters. It was right in the center of town and had three firefighters and the duty officer.

Years back, when we still staffed our own dispatch desk, when someone was out we had to cover shifts man for man, and I guess it seemed expensive to the powers that be. So, they and the chief started looking for ways to cut the overtime costs.

One of the first ideas that they came up with was when someone was out, instead of filling the vacancy with an overtime shift for someone, they would have one firefighter from station 2 and the duty officer from station 1 both switch stations. The duty officer would work with the other firefighter at station 2, and station 1 would run a man short that shift. This arrangement lasted for one winter, maybe about three months, and it was only during nights and weekends. The duty officer has a lot to do at station 1 during the workday.

I remember working a night at station 2 with the deputy of the department, just the two of us. Conversation didn't exactly flow, not that I didn't like him. He was fine, but I was intimidated being as new as I was. I felt better the next morning when I woke to the sound of a bell ringing and realized that it was the doorbell. I heard hurried movement from the next room where the deputy had spent the night. I looked at the clock and it was a quarter to eight in the morning. We would be off duty in fifteen minutes and we were just waking up! The rules were that we had to be up by 7:00 and clean the engine and anything else we had used. It had been a quiet night and so we slept almost all night.

The doorbell was being rung by the guys on the incoming shift trying to get in the firehouse. The door was still locked. This was kind of a rare thing. I was usually awake no later than

6:30, but not today! Today I slept late in front of the deputy...but what the hell; he slept late, too, so nothing was ever said.

Another thing that made that winter memorable was that the captain on my shift, who was a pain in the ass, worked nights and weekends at station 2 for almost the whole winter. That left just three of us at headquarters. We had all grown up and gone to school together and had been friends. We all knew the job and did it well, without immediate supervision, so we had a great time. There was lots of laughing and pranks.

One of us took a chance and went to bed early one night. A short while after he went to sleep, the other guy and I went and got the masks out of two SCBA cases. We put them on and went into the bunkroom and knelt down next to the guy's bed and got right in his face with the masks on. Something from another dimension must have spoken to him as he slowly woke and looked at the two things staring at him. He screamed and was scared to death. We started to laugh and soon the guy was laughing with us. No one dared to go to bed early after that, and we stayed up until all of us were tired.

One night, we heard one guy get up to use the can, so the other guy and I went and sat on the guy's bed until he came back. The light was off and as he tried to get into bed, we pounced. He yelled and jumped back, much to our amusement.

After that winter, other budget-cutting measures were explored and things changed. Sometime after that, we started using civilian dispatchers, and so we didn't need to put a man on the desk so we could run a man short if someone was out. I think us firefighters did better as dispatchers, but the civilians were here to stay and we never had another winter like that!

Coffee...Our Life's Blood

Many people start their day off with a nice hot cuppa Joe. I don't know why they call it Joe, or for that matter, who *they* are, anyway. At the firehouse, there was coffee on all the time and guys drank it at night. If you have to be up in the dead of night in the cold winter, a hot coffee is a great companion. The town provided the firehouse and the kitchen, but the firefighters provide their own coffee and drip coffee makers.

When I was on the job, we had a coffee fund. I joined it when I was a call firefighter. It cost five dollars a month for all the coffee you wanted (including the fixin's), or you could pay for it by the cup. I don't remember the cost per cup, but five bucks a month was a good deal.

Well, as prices went up, so did the monthly cost of the fund. At first, snacks, condiments, butter, crackers, sardines, and an assortment of other things were also bought with the fund, but most of the snacks were discontinued. Coupled with the occasional person who took and intended to pay later, but never did, the snacks were a losing proposition.

Several people had been in control of the fund, which meant that that person collected and held the money and did the shopping. I remember thinking what a pain in the ass that job must be. There was never too much money left after the shopping was done, and there was not too much that was bought.

One time, the fund was in danger of being disbanded when the one in charge wanted out of the responsibility and couldn't find anyone who was willing to take over. That person got tired of having a few vocal people constantly complain about how things were done. So, after some pressure, I took the job.

The past fund managers always had to chase people for money. There was very little surplus money given to me when I took over the fund and not enough to shop. After I collected money from everyone, I had quite a bit of money. Then I went shopping. I really don't like to shop. I know what I want before I go in and buy it. A problem was the storage of what I bought. I could only buy so much. But I'm pretty good with money and I bought whatever coffee was on sale and I bought a whole case of it in the box. I bought a case of creamer and a few pounds of sugar, lots of butter, salt, pepper, and condiments. I bought all the necessities and filled the cabinets and the fridge, and you know what? I didn't spent half of the money I had available. I shopped about once a month and never had to chase people for money because I always had plenty in the fund, and also because for some reason, most paid without being asked, often a month or more in advance.

I did have some run-ins with the complainers and naysayers. I made the mortal sin of buying dish detergent and one guy was loud and nasty about that. He insisted that the town should pay for that. Didn't seem like a big deal to me, so I kept it up. That guy cornered me in the kitchen one day and proceeded to yell at me and tell me *not* to buy dish soap.

Well, I remember casually standing and looking him straight in the eye and telling him, "If you want to do the shopping, I'll give you the money."

He replied, "You aren't gonna give me shit!"

I told him to shut his piehole and leave me alone. He was the only one that ever gave me any real crap, and that put an end to it. There's no point yelling if no one is listening.

We always had plenty of money and people paid more or less on time. I never found it to be a pain in the butt—except for the jerks who mouthed off—and I was a better shopper and the cupboards were full.

Then, I got promoted to lieutenant and had to go to station 2 where they had their own fund. I gave up the job and the fund went right back to the way it was before me: broke and running out of things. Oh well, not my concern anymore!

Some Nasty Shit

There are many flammable gasses. They are in use everywhere, every day, for many things. We cook and heat our homes with natural gas or propane, which is a petroleum product. Those are the gasses that I have experience with in the residential community where I worked. There is always butane, but I'm told that that is used where the weather is warm all year due to a slight difference in properties. So I have experience with what we use here in Massachusetts.

There are natural gas mains and services under our yards and streets. Natural gas is cooled to liquefy it. It's cooled to a temperature below -260°F, so a spill of that stuff not only is flammable, but cold enough to kill. Those kinds of things happen most often in transportation accidents. Since my town had no direct access to the nearby interstate, I didn't see those too often, but there was always the problem in homes or businesses with gas leaks from appliances and such.

A construction crew digging up a gas pipe is pretty common. Most contractors seem to know what to do when the backhoe catches one. The rule is to pull it up out of the hole and let it free flow into the air, and then stop the flow and get it fixed. Natural gas is lighter than air, so when the pipe is pulled out of the hole, the gas tends to rise and dissipate.

It's bad when natural gas fills a house or a building where there are people. It is an asphyxiating gas, as well as a flammable one. I've seen houses literally blown to bits from a gas explosion, and I even saw an entire house turned on its foundation because of an explosion.

Sometime in the late 60s to early 70s, the gas grill became popular. Before long, nearly everyone had at least a twenty-pound tank of propane attached to the grill, and often another tank stored away–all full of gas, of course.

Propane is a gas that deserves respect and bears watching. It is heavier than air, and so it settles in low places, like storm drains and basements. It's transported in liquid form after pressurizing. Being under pressure, a propane leak can shoot out, and the stuff is explosively flammable. If an ignition source is found by the expanding vapor, the whole thing will ignite and burn back to the source extremely fast. In addition to grills, propane is used to heat pools, pool houses, sheds, and appliances inside homes, as well as the homes themselves.

I worked with propane for years, and through teaching about it, I got pretty familiar with it. Still, I took any classes I could to learn more about it, as well as to train on commanding an incident of a gas leak or explosion. As training officer, I also got gas training for the members of my fire department. As a small department, we had limited resources, but there was still a lot we could do if there was a leak.

Well, sure enough, one day it happened. We had just gotten a new chief not long before and he was at a meeting when the call came in for a full, one-hundred-pound propane tank that had blown its valve and was free flowing. It was in a residential neighborhood. The lieutenant from station 2 got there first and knew just what he was doing. I got there, signed off in command, and had the engine that had come from station 1 establish a water supply.

When the chief arrived a short time later, I walked up the street to meet him in full gear and gave him a report. I told him that we had a water supply established and had two small lines fully extended and charged. Houses nearby had been evacuated, and checks were being made with the gas detection meters. The chief just kind of looked and shrugged his shoulders.

He said something like, "What do you need me here for?" and he went back to his meeting.

Who the hell needed the boss? We had this! There turned out not to be a fire, but all these precautions were necessary. Let loose from its cage, that propane is some nasty shit!

The Black Hole

The staff at the state fire academy was a mixture of men and women from across the state, from cities and small town fire departments. The instructors in the recruit program brought many stories of calls that they went on. It was interesting to hear all those people from different places tell their stories. But there was one town that seemed to attract disaster more than the rest.

We had an instructor who was a captain from that town. He was pretty well thought of. He was a good lecturer, knowledgeable, and a pretty good guy. It seemed that whenever someone told a story about something, that captain would tell about the time that the same thing happened in his town: not stories of his own exploits, just stories of the incidents. Maybe he was just pulling someone's chain, but it happened so frequently that it became comical. People started saying that all that could be heard from that town was screaming, gunfire, and sounds of explosions. They talked about being afraid to travel through that town in case catastrophes were to strike. It was a running joke. I dubbed the place the "Black Hole of Catastrophe."

One night, my wife and I sketched out a "tourist" map of that town. That is to say, I made up things to put there and my wife, who has all the drawing talent, drew. Included were roads and walking paths leading to such attractions as the unexploded ordinance or the UFO landing site. There was a uranium cave and land mines, hazardous materials spills, and a polluted river flowing from the mountains where dwelt the Yeti. There was an international airport with its fuel spills and crashes, a major sea port with an approaching tsunami, and a terrorist training camp. There were major fires burning, including one engulfing the combined orphanage and puppy shelter. Mayhem was the order of the day.

When it was completed, I rolled up the map and brought it in the next time I went to work at the academy. I always got there early. I was the first one there and I set the map, still rolled up, on the table in the ready room, and said nothing as others found their way into the room. The room was filling up fast when someone noticed the rolled paper on the table. They asked about it, but no one knew anything.

So, someone picked it up and unrolled it. It was an instant hit. People loved it and laughed hard. Then they started asking where it had come from, and who had left it there. No one would admit any knowledge of the thing...not even me.

They started to narrow down the list of suspects. They had one guy who they liked for it, but he wasn't there that day. Then someone inspecting the map closely noticed some graffiti written on the wall of a cave. It was two sets of initials written inside of a heart. One set happened to be the same as my initials. They started to ask me specific questions, like what my wife's first name was, and though I denied knowing anything, I think that I was a major suspect. I don't know who they finally gave the credit to.

The day ended, and the map disappeared. There is a rumor that the guy from the town in question took it home. He isn't the type to be pissed. He laughed as hard as anyone. Besides, it was a great idea and fine artwork, if I do say so myself!

Rocket Man

The town where I worked has a river running through it and there is a pond that supposedly feeds into the river. The old maps show a small stream connecting the pond to the river, but I've never seen it. The river is polluted now, a victim of industrial waste, but I can remember swimming and fishing there years ago.

The pond is very murky and weedy, not too good for swimming, but as for fishing, that is another matter. It is full of hornpout, and though I've never tried it, I'm told that it's a good fish to eat.

The pond was a very popular place with fishermen, and not just local fishermen, either. It was very popular with people who would drive out from the city any nice weekend. The woods would be full of people fishing.

I never really thought that those people were into fishing. My grandfather told me that he was fishing there once and caught a whole bunch of hornpout. As he stood there, some people came out of the woods and asked how his luck was. Granddad said it was going great. He pulled up his line of fish out of the water to show them what he had already caught. When he saw the envious looks he got, he gave the fish to the men. They were very thankful, and didn't stick around. They got in their car and went home. They had the fish they wanted without having to be bothered fishing!

Many people coming from the city to fish would bring a boat with them. The problem with the city folk is that they often aren't too good with boats, and all too often, they can't swim. Plus, like fishermen the world over, they bring their booze with them—sometimes beer, but often someone would break out a bottle of brandy or some other liquor. That really added another element.

All too often, the fishermen would be half shot and trying to get too many people into a boat that wasn't big enough. As more people climbed on board, someone would get bumped and fall over the side. Maybe someone would get hit by a paddle or an oar being waved around by another person. Tempers would flare in the sun, and when you add in plenty of booze, soon there might be a fight and someone would go over the side.

One day, many years ago, when I was a call firefighter, a boatload of city guys set off into the pond. They had their necessary equipment, including their hooch. They were probably pretty drunk when a fight broke out. One guy fell into the water and sunk out of sight. He didn't come back up, so his friends went to call for help. As cell phones hadn't been invented yet, they had to row to the bank and get to a phone. There wasn't much hope of a quick rescue for the guy under the water.

At that time, the fire department had what they called a dive team made up of a few men who were scuba divers. There were no formal drills and no special training. In short, they were an underwater recovery group.

The dive team reported to the pond for the missing boater. One of the divers who showed up was a guy I had grown up with. We both got on the call department together. I thought I knew him pretty well, but until that time, I never knew he was a diver.

Into that murky water a couple of divers slid from a fire department boat. They started feeling around for the victim. At some point, my buddy was feeling around when his hand grasped something he didn't expect; it was the hand of the drowning victim. They say that my buddy shot up out of the water like a missile, took a couple steps on the water, and landed in the boat. Embellishment is a time honored skill with story tellers on the fire department, but I'm not sure if it was used here. I think I would have done the same thing.

After some years, that dive team just disappeared. It was replaced by something the police threw together that wasn't any better. I only ever worked with them a couple of times and I never saw them do anything but scan just under the surface. I never saw any of those cops actually dive underwater completely, so they found nothing ever. At least our Rocket Man found what he was looking for!

He Wasn't Worried

I worked for a small suburban fire department that was an all-call department until the mid 50s. There was a major fire one winter, and after that, the town decided to staff the two firehouses with full-time people. They appointed four guys...two for each station.

One of the men hired for station 1 was the man I replaced when I came on full-time. He lived about a mile from the firehouse. He was a firefighter, the department mechanic, and a pilot who built his own airplane in the firehouse. He was quiet and soft spoken. I am told that he was kind of an old farmer type.

A deputy that I worked with had also worked with him back when he came on the department. That deputy loved to tell stories and he got along well with the old timer.

Well, one morning the future deputy, always an early riser, got up at the firehouse to find the man missing. He looked everywhere and couldn't locate him. He didn't really know what to do, but a short time later, the old timer came walking back up the street and back to the firehouse like nothing had happened. He said that one of his neighbors had called and told him that his cows had gotten out of the pasture, so he had gone and walked home and took his cows back to the pasture then walked back, just as if it was something he did every day. He had no portable radio with him, either.

When his partner expressed some concern, he answered something like, "Did you get any calls when I was gone?"

Hearing the word "No," he said, "Then don't worry about it."

Nothing was ever said about it, though the tale lingers on. Life was simpler then. You couldn't get away with that shit now!

Who's the Teacher?

I was in the fire service for a long time, (thirty-three years, in fact), and in my day, everybody had a side job. After trying my hand at a great many things, I realized that firefighting was the only thing I knew how to do well, so I went to work at the state firefighting academy. The administrative staff works there full-time, but all the teaching is done by active or retired firefighters on their days off from their fire departments. Though the recruit program is the heart and soul of the place, the academy offers many different courses in the many different aspects of the fire service. From chief officers to recruit firefighters, there is something for everybody.

Of course, as with every group, some instructors are better than others. There are some who have no business teaching, but for the most part, the instruction is good. Trouble is, when they send an instructor to teach a course, they don't always send the best, most logical person: the person with real life expertise that doesn't just come out of a book. A bunch of us only taught the recruit program to make sure the guys that replaced us would know what they're doing. I taught the flammable gas program, too. Since just about everyone has propane for their grills, it's a good idea to stay sharp with it.

There are many programs, some that are geared toward career and call firefighters and others for volunteers. I think the academy's idea was to have everybody ready to teach everything so they can send out anybody to teach anything. Well, that's a great idea, in theory, but it's a fact of life that if you don't use it on your job, then you have to learn it from a book. That's OK, too, but veteran firefighters usually already know something of what you're teaching, and you can't fool a bunch of veteran firefighters. If you don't really know what you are talking about, they can pick out a line of bullshit in a heartbeat. They want a teacher who understands what they have to deal with. It's easier to really take something in from someone who has some actual experience with a subject, than to hear it from someone who just learned from a book. Hell...I can buy the book, too!

There is a story of a small city not too far off. If memory serves, they scheduled a program on high rise operations. I heard that the department getting the course told the academy to send someone with experience, someone from someplace where they do high rise operations. So who did they send? A man that wasn't even a full-time firefighter, much less someone with any experience in high rise buildings. I hear that the guys asked the instructor where he was from. When he told them, they were very upset and cancelled the class. To me, it only made sense to send the most qualified instructor, the guy with not only a title, but with experience to back it up.

Yes, we're all firefighters, but where you work affects the kind of things you do. You can't expect a city firefighter to have experience with rural firefighting or a part-time firefighter from a small town to have high rise experience. Where I worked–with the recruits–we taught the basics of firefighting, the meat of the job. Every recruit instructor should be skilled in this. The only problem is whether they can teach or not. Not everyone has the gift.

In the 90s, something called Rapid Intervention Teams was developed. These RIT teams were trained to rescue trapped firefighters. A team was to be designated at a fire and stand by unless and until they were needed. Too many firefighters were getting killed. It's a dangerous business, but RIT teams gave some hope to firefighters trapped in a burning building.

At first, our academy didn't have a RIT lesson plan, so I went to another academy, not too far from me, to learn it. That academy also offered a structural collapse course and a technical rescue program that were great. I got into the RIT program. It was a very intense weekend learning about firefighter rescue under fire conditions, including self rescue and much more. The course was taught by a heavy rescue company from a busy city department to the south of us. It was a hardworking weekend and a lot of learning was done. I was beat, but I loved it.

When I heard that our academy had developed a RIT program a while later, I made a call and got my department on the schedule. I had high hopes, but I was apprehensive. Come the day the class started, in walked three of the very last people I would have picked to teach this. I knew them all, and not one had any real-life experience with any RIT team. This was the most unbelievable example of the wrong staff being sent out to teach a course. It was terrible! Now they teach RIT in recruit training, and it's quality instruction. That other program was eventually scrapped, I guess. At least, I never heard of it again.

The academy did it to me again when I scheduled a class for my department on handling a gas incident. We had an instructor from a nearby town who we all knew and didn't think too highly of. He just wanted to come to our firehouse to show off. They could have sent someone who was very familiar with the subject; the academy has all those people on staff. They just don't seem to understand that they need to send the right ones.

Other things I've thought about include wondering who the hell trained the real old time people. There were several instructors that seemed to be at the academy certifying everybody else to teach. I just can't help but wonder who taught and certified them? I guess I'll never know.

There was something that I heard was being established where I think they were dead wrong to get involved, and they picked the worst people possible to run the program. I am a recovering alcoholic. As of this writing, I have been twenty-seven years sober. I talk about it often as part of my recovery. In the course of my conversations, I heard that the academy, or its parent department within the state, had established a program of help for firefighters with alcohol problems. Sounds like a great idea, right? Well true to form, they had the wrong people running it.

One was a guy I'd met a few years before. He worked in the administrative offices with the big shots, but he was in the yard one day in his business suit. He asked me about my work, where I worked, for how long, and stuff like that. He put his hand out to shake, and as I shook his hand, I saw a hand that had never done a hard day's work in all his life. He told me that he was a retired deputy from a small all-call department a ways west of me. I don't know much about this guy, but he sure as hell wasn't a firefighter. He had office hands. So now I know this guy is full of shit. I saw him often and was cordial, but my opinion hadn't changed.

One year he decided he wanted to get himself a chief's job to help boost his retirement pay. He got a job as chief of an island community. It's supposed to be a great place in the summer when the tourists swarm there, but deadly dull off season. It takes a certain kind of person to live in a place like that. It seems that our friend wasn't cut out for that life. He developed a drinking problem and got himself fired in less than a year.

There are no secrets in the fire service. Everybody heard what happened...but the guy came back to the academy and strutted around a bit. So naturally, because he had some problems with his drinking and was apparently now an expert, they put him as one of the two in charge of that program. He has a line of BS like a salesman trying to sell you something. I wouldn't have gone to him anyway, but I also knew his story. I didn't consider him a firefighter brother. I know a great many people, but I can't think of any that would go and discuss their problems with this guy.

The other guy in charge was also someone who shouldn't have been put in charge of anything, and the academy knew it. He had been in charge of several programs through the years and had gotten fired from every one for not knowing what he was doing. I don't know why they thought he was a good man for this job. His reputation is well-known also, and the stories get told and spread...and the memories are long. Another fabulous choice!

Lividity

All fire departments have people that they see again and again when they respond with the ambulance. There are, of course, those abusers of the system, but most are really in need of help when they call.

I remember one lady that we saw many times through the years. I don't recall what the exact problem was, but she was bedridden and I don't think I ever saw her coherent. She was the wife of a town selectman and she had a caretaker. She was familiar to us not because she had frequent problems, but rather that we had known her for so long. Over the years, we had watched her decline.

We hadn't seen her for a long while when we got a call to go to her house with the ambulance. We were met in the driveway by the caretaker who told us that the lady was deceased. I asked if there was a DNR order in place, expecting the answer to be "Yes," seeing as they had so long to prepare for this as her condition declined. Imagine my shock when the caretaker didn't know what I was talking about. I explained the law requiring us to do CPR on the patient in the absence of a DNR (as long as there aren't any contraindications, in which case we would not start CPR).

She was shocked and begged us not to begin to work on the lady. It didn't sound right to me, either. I asked the caretaker to take us in. I found pretty much what I expected. There was a long-time bedridden elderly woman that had no pulse. The caretaker was watching me anxiously as I pulled the sheets and blanket aside to look at the patient. I didn't need any imagination. There it was...the lividity I was looking for, a contraindication to performing CPR. The lady had been gone too long, and anyway, it would have seemed criminal to work her. May she rest in peace.

Oops...

In 1964, my department started a Christmas tradition. We send Santa Claus out on a fire engine over three nights, and have a schedule of stops where Santa will meet with and talk to the kids. It was popular and continues to this day with each new generation of kids.

We mount Santa's sleigh atop a fire engine and fasten it down, install a sound system for Christmas music and Santa's microphone, plus add all the lights needed to see Santa up on his sleigh. When the kids gather around to sit on his lap, we light up the area so no one gets hurt. The power for all these electronics comes from the engine. It's quite a draw, so we used to put the engine on a charger for the night between rides. Nowadays there are extension cords on spools and quick disconnect plugs and receptacles. Back then, we plugged an extension cord in the wall and ran it across the floor to the battery charger.

The first stop for Santa is at 1700 hours each night. We try to keep to the schedule. One year, a bunch of us got to the firehouse early to make sure things were ready to go. While we waited, a report of a house fire came in. The deputy kept telling us that he only wanted the on-duty crew to respond, but we pretended not to hear and got on the step and rode to the fire. The fire really cut things close with sticking to Santa's schedule, but we got back with a short time to spare before the ride started.

With us that afternoon was a guy that I had come on the job with—sort of. He came on about seven months before me, but the same year. This guy was one of a line of firefighters from his family. His father was an officer on our department. He'd been around for a long time, and some of the older guys didn't care for the old man, so they busted the kid's balls. He really used to get wound up.

Well, the department mechanic was on duty that day and was checking Santa's engine. (He was also a guy that shared a mutual hatred of both father and son, and they didn't care for him, either.) After returning from the fire, we quickly got ready to take Santa. My buddy got in the cab to pull the engine out.

There was someone watching and helping him back out. Suddenly, there was a <*crunch*> and a dragging sound. He stopped the engine and several people looked under, including the mechanic.

There, under the engine, was the battery charger, somewhat flatter than it used to be. The mechanic was apoplectic as he yelled insults at the driver. That driver was just so cranked up and stressed that he was shaking and clutching the steering wheel. The whole scene was just comical with these guys screaming at each other. All the other people there got a big kick out of things.

Well, we got out in time to drive Santa around, a new battery charger had to be bought, and I hope the two guys had a merry Christmas!

Learning Never Stops

I started in emergency services in 1974. I became a call firefighter, went to a training academy, and the next year I got into EMT school. My training academy was fun, but I don't remember being anything but confused as the guys who taught us about things like pumps and building construction really didn't know how to teach it. I learned what I could there, and on the job, for my first few years. I didn't have anyone to really work with me on things.

As for EMT work, I learned something every time I went out, and got pretty good at what I did. I spent a while working per diem for a private ambulance. They did a different type of call from the fire ambulance. The fire ambulance did emergency work, but the private ambulance companies did routine transports of sick people. There was a lot to learn about communication and moving people of all shapes and sizes. I took my time and watched the ones who hurt themselves moving people, and those who didn't, and saw why and how. I learned.

At one point, there was some union trouble between the ambulance company and the firefighters' union, and I had to stop working for the ambulance company for a while. The trouble quieted down, but the bad feelings did not. There was always one particular mouthy guy from the fire department telling me that I shouldn't work for a private ambulance company. But, I did stay and kept learning.

Guys on my own fire department thought that the privates were a home for idiots and the like. I never found that to be true. The wealth of knowledge I got and applied to my jobs, both at the ambulance company and the fire department, was huge. I know several guys in the firehouse who have hurt backs and shoulders and necks from lifting someone improperly. These guys didn't want to hear it from me; after all, I worked with the privates. I didn't hurt myself because I learned to do things right.

I remember one call when I was the officer in charge. It was at an elderly housing community. The engine was there before me. When I walked in, I saw a very large, elderly woman seated on the floor. My two guys were trying to get her to her feet by pulling her up. They weren't having any success. The lady wasn't hurt; she just needed help into a chair. I walked behind the lady and explained what I was doing. I squatted behind her, wrapped my arms around her, and took hold of her wrists. I pulled her really close and slowly stood up, bringing her with me. When she was up, the other guys dragged a chair over and we sat her in it.

She said, "Thanks," and the other guys looked at me like I had done something magic. It was just another thing learned in the private ambulance service.

I already had twelve years on the job when I started working at the academy. I had some knowledge of pumps and things, but it was there, working in a support position, that the fire learning really started. I learned what I could, and kept learning as I taught firefighting and everything that it entails. Then after some years, I was a senior instructor and was often a lead instructor or the burn commander...and learning continued. Each time I sent a crew into a fire, I thought of a scenario and a battle plan, and watched as the recruits attacked the fire. Watching them, I learned a great deal, and was able to pass some things I observed to future classes.

There was a guy I worked with at the academy who worked for a town near mine. He was a pretty good guy, but talked a bit too much, and so it was said that a little bit of him went a long way. I had been at the academy longer than him, but he advanced to instructor a bit before I did. Not being a social climbing sort, I was happy to stay working support for a while. When I did become an instructor, this guy, ever the sort to flaunt his meager experience to the new guy, told me that he couldn't wait until I did my first lecture. I guess he was going to heckle me, but I reminded him that I'd been doing lectures in EMS classes since before I had ever heard of him. He didn't heckle me then–or ever.

One day, the guy came up to me at the burn building between burns. He told me that they thought I did a nice job and he asked me where I had learned all the things I knew. He half said and half asked if I had learned all that on the fire department in my town. I guess I did...every time I went to work!

Sticking Around

Driving through the town the other day, I spotted my old elementary school. I looked up and saw something that really took me back...to where, I'm not really sure. If you look on the south side of the building facing the main street, there is a big section of blank wall. On that wall there is a splat of something stuck on it. It looks like it could be mud. The thing is, there used to be two of them. I was there when they were thrown up against the wall and stuck. I really had to cut through all the debris and flotsam and jetsam in my memory, then sweep away some of the dust and moss, to remember.

I couldn't tell you how old I was, but I was young, early grammar-school-age young. I have a pretty vivid picture in my mind of a group of kids with their bikes on that side of the school. I don't remember who any of them were, except me. One of them threw a handful of something up onto the wall and it stuck. Then he did it again. It might have been mud.

Well, that stuff has been up there ever since. I would look at it from time to time when I went to that school, and I've see it sometimes through the years. I always remembered being there when it was thrown there.

One of the balls of mud is gone now. Don't know when it fell off, but the other one is still there. It's been there more than 50 years! I know this is a lot of drivel to most of you, but I haven't thought of that day for many years now, and seeing the mud kind of brought me back to another time.

Keeping the Job

Firefighter jobs are hard to get, and for every malcontent there have to be a hundred who would sell their soul for the job. The entry process usually involves a test of some kind, often a general intelligence test or a job specific test with study material. There is usually a physical fitness test, too. Then it's onto the list you go until it's your turn and a job opens up. Get the job, and it's off to a training academy for basic training. Then you have a probationary period to go through: usually a year, during which time the probie is watched and drilled. He's watched to see how well he works with the other guys and learns and follows direction. He also gets whatever training is needed for additional things, like EMT or paramedic. During the probation period, a guy can be let go for any reason. If everything is done right, the probie will have a job for his or her working career, unless money problems in the town or city force layoffs. But sometimes other things go wrong and a guy is dismissed.

There has been a "No smoking" law in effect for years now that prohibits any police officer or firefighter from smoking 24 hours a day throughout his career. The penalty for breaking the law is termination. I don't know how many guys might have lost their jobs because of smoking; must be some, but I don't know of any.

I have seen a few people lose their jobs because they couldn't pass the recruit training at the academy. Distressing, but the job isn't for everyone. There was a recruit once from a city to our west who showed up looking great. He was athletic-looking and jacked. He had also graduated from college, where he had played football. Well, it was found that the guy couldn't do the basic math required for pump operation. He didn't listen and started to accumulate a large number of demerits for his poor performances. As demerits accumulate, there are two times when the recruit has a meeting with his chief and the recruit coordinator. At one of these meetings, the recruit complained that the instructors were picking on him because he was black. The guy's chief knew that he was trying to blame everyone else for his lack of learning and fired him on the spot.

As training officer, I was responsible for the call firefighters. I did cause several of them to be let go, but as a full-time firefighter, I only saw two men terminated. One was a guy who came from town and everyone knew him. His family went way back and his father had held a prominent position in town government. There was a money crunch in town at that time. There was an open firefighter position that would be filled, but the person getting the job would not be going to the academy for training. At that time, when the fire department hired someone, they would send him to EMT school, but the probie had to pass the course and have his EMT certification by the time his probation was up. This guy got himself into an EMT course. Trouble was, he wouldn't study. Even during quiet time at the station he could be seen with a coffee and a cigarette walking around and shooting the bull, but not studying.

He also had a rare opportunity. Due to some changes to the EMS agencies, the guy was able to take the national EMT test instead of the state test. He failed. Then he got to take the state test...and failed. He was able to take a retest of the state exam...and he failed that, too. With no more tests to take and no more time to take another class before his probation period ended, there was no choice, no matter who he was. He saw it coming and resigned. The town learned a lesson: hire people who are already EMTs.

The other guy was the kind of guy that you want to get rid of before real trouble starts. He didn't listen or follow orders and didn't get along with the other firefighters or the officers. He was like that as a student in the academy. Yes, he had an academy diploma. He had been on two other fire departments before coming to us. Both had let him go before his probie year was up. The second department that hired him sent him to the academy where I got a chance to see him first hand. He didn't listen, never seemed to understand, though one would look at him and see that he wasn't straining to learn. I was still teaching at that time, but I had retired from the firehouse when this guy was hired by my old department. I did some talking and found that the people there didn't like him at all. The chief, at that time, was a guy that generally tried to keep his own ass free from any controversy. The guy in question was black...not African American, but based on his accent, from a Caribbean island somewhere. Well, if he wanted to make a racial issue out of it, it could get messy and that chief didn't want that. The guy also had a diploma from the academy and had his paramedic certificate. He was a terrible student and I don't know how he scraped by, but he did. If he was kept around, it scares me to think that he was going to be on the street treating patients as a paramedic. It got to the last week of the man's probation and the guys on the department were getting desperate. I figured that that chief would do what he had to do to keep his own ass in the clear. The officers finally had a serious sit down with the chief and got him to change his mind. The chief let him go. Never thought he'd do that. I'm glad I was wrong.

Number Please

The town I worked in wasn't very big at all. It is roughly six miles long by about five miles or so wide. The population hovers around fourteen thousand. We had no 911 system in place at first. The residents were expected to dial the seven digit number or go through the operator. Here's where some problems started. Our town had its own phone exchange, but we also used phone exchanges from neighboring towns for locations near the town borders. An operator might send an emergency call to the wrong town's fire department, delaying the response. Even that would have worked fine—except for the callers. People will say some strange things when under stress and scared. I once had a lady with a fire in her kitchen forget her own address. Many people's minds just don't work right in times of trouble.

One night, I was on duty and was sitting at the dispatch desk, when the dispatcher from the town to our south called and asked if we had a certain street in our town. I answered, "Yes," and they gave me the house number. First of all, the street was the one I lived on, and second, the address was very familiar to me. It was my neighbors. They said the call was for the ambulance for a gunshot wound. That isn't something we like to hear. I haven't dealt with too many gunshot wounds, but those I've seen were pretty bad. I got the south side engine dispatched with about a thirty second response time and got the ambulance started.

Responding companies reported an adult female with a small caliber gunshot wound to the buttocks...I don't remember which one. It seems that she was the victim of a pistol that fired while it was being cleaned. I'm a gun owner and a shooter. I have been for years, and I just can't figure out how you clean a pistol while it's loaded and ready to fire. The incident became a police matter after the patient was cared for and taken to the hospital. The lady was very lucky. Even a small caliber can kill easily.

We did have another accidental discharge of a revolver involving a police officer. I wasn't present, but the story was told to me by the police officer himself some years later. This cop was a guy who grew up in town, and had been on the police department for a number of years when the revolver that he car- carried went off and shot him in the leg. I don't know just how you do that, but the wound was bad and he was hospitalized. He received a blood transfusion, which he said was the reason he came down with the diabetes that plagued him for the rest of his life. He tried to stay on the job, but he grew progressively worse over the years. He had to retire when his eyesight failed. That gunshot wound resulted in his death many years afterwards.

I don't know how you clean a loaded gun, but some people try anyway.

Memory Lapse

On my job, we didn't get too many opportunities to do live burn training, but we got a number of houses slated to be torn down and used them to drill on the many other things we do at fires. We raised ladders, opened walls and roofs, practiced search and rescue, to name a few. But when we got a place to burn, we tried to make the most of it.

Some years ago, we did manage to get a place. We held two evenings of live burns on two steamy July nights. The heat and humidity were unbelievable. I was the igniter, as I had some experience with live fire training. I was inside the house for every fire. I built them, setting up wood and straw to burn, then lit them and made sure they were burning properly before making my way out. The drill was great, as all live fire training is.

For the finale, I built a kitchen fire. Mind you...I *know* how to build a fire, and I did this kitchen fire right. The idea was to let the fire get going well, and then have the hose crew enter into the room with heavy fire and put it out. This fire was supposed to be the best and biggest one of all. I got it lit, spread the fire around to get the whole room involved, and went out through the back door. I walked around front, where I planned to watch the crew going in after giving the fire enough time to really get going. I started to take off my gear just in time to see a captain in charge of a hose line panic and start his crew in too early and all but ruin my masterpiece!

Well, that evening I was supposed to be on duty, as was the captain who ruined my last fire. We were given the time off to work at the burn...me, because I was the igniter; him, because...who knows? But we still had to get cleaned up after the burn and report to headquarters for duty. I went to the south side station to clean up and shower. I think I had about an inch of liquid sweat clinging to my body, and ashes and straw stuck in every orifice. Man, that hot water felt good. Then I heard the stall next to me spring to life as the water came on. I was about done when I heard a voice from the next stall. It was that captain's voice asking me if I had an extra bar of soap. He said he didn't have any.

I thought a bit, then looked at the two bars of soap in my stall, and told him, "Yes, there are two bars. I only washed my ass with one of them."

He replied, "Yea, and you can't remember which one..."

To which I replied something like, "Ya hit that one on the head Capt...I just can't remember. Sorry."

I left and went to work. The captain showed up a while after, all cleaned up. Wonder where he got the soap. He never said.

People

People in the fire service are just ordinary people, except they share a passion for firefighting, rescue, sirens, and danger. Otherwise, they're just like everyone else with their likes and dislikes, hopes, fears, concerns, as well as a capacity for incredible courage and unbelievable stupidity.

Not too long ago, I worked with two men at the firefighting academy. These guys were from the same fire department and worked the same shift, one as a senior officer, the other as a junior officer. The junior officer was a good friend of mine. The other one was a guy I knew from work, but I wasn't really friends with him.

One day, my friend seemed really bothered by something. After some talk, he told me a story. It seems that recently, on one of their night shifts, the junior officer had caught a glimpse of the senior officer, and he was getting a pedicure from a female firefighter—and a probie at that. They didn't know that they were seen, and my friend was really bothered by what he'd witnessed.

Now, I have no doubt that the officer wouldn't have let anything go further...his wife would kill him. Further, I don't think he pulled the old, "Cause I'm the boss, that's why!" It was just playing around, incredibly stupid playing around–yes, it sure was.

But, appearances are key; this was a probie female firefighter and the senior shift officer alone in a room with a pedicure going on. If the media ever got ahold of that, imagine what they would do with it! That's an example of inappropriate firehouse behavior that could cost the whole department and the fire service their reputation, and that's one thing no one wants to lose.

The junior officer was the one who told me the story. He didn't want things to get ugly if the incident was brought into the open. People could have lost their jobs, and the damage to the public perception of the department could have been drastic.

My buddy swore me to secrecy, and I never spoke of it–until now. But, it makes for a good story of what should not go on. All the individuals involved are gone. The two officers have long since retired, and from what I understand, the female firefighter involved did not make it through probation. I don't know why she was let go, but a probie can be let go any time during the probationary period for just about anything.

As far as I know, nothing was ever made of that incident. My friend chose to keep things quiet for the good of everyone. I'm not sure I would have handled it the same way, but that's something I never had to worry about.

Lamont

I remember many moons ago when the town hall housed both the fire and police departments in the same building. It was that way when I first came to the fire department. We always had people walking in front of our bay doors going to and from the town hall...citizens and employees alike.

There was a man who worked for the town engineer that I saw often and got to know. He was a temporary employee...a rather tall, black man–no, not African American. He was from Costa Rica and spoke heavily accented English, but was good enough with it to carry on a conversation. And, converse we did–often.

As we got more familiar, he used to come into the firehouse and sit with me and tell me about his country and what life was like there. He even brought me food on occasion, like mangoes and other assorted things that he had at home. Sure, he could have bought the mango at Stop and Shop, but the fact remains that they grow in Costa Rica and I had never had one.

Back then, many of us smoked, including me. My friend used to bring me cigarettes from Costa Rica that his friends and family would send him. (I still remember the name of the cigarettes. They were called Capri.) I got to know the guy pretty well.

At that time, I had hair. (Now I'm bald.) It was very curly and it spawned nicknames for me. I worked with a man who grew up in the segregated south. He would compare my hair with that of black people. There was a show on TV then called "Sanford and Son." It was a sitcom with the stars being black people, and so my group at the firehouse called me "Lamont," after one of the characters, and the name stuck for a while.

Eventually, my friend's job came to an end, and so did the stream of people walking in front of our doors after the town hall moved elsewhere.

Now fast forward about twenty-five years. I was a lieutenant and on duty at station 2. We always had people coming in asking for directions. One day, as we stood in front of the bay door looking out the window, someone came in. My partner went to see what he wanted. It was a black man and that's all I noticed as my partner talked to him. The man turned and left, and we continued to look out at the street.

Shortly, I asked my partner what that man had wanted. He told me that he just was looking for someone. Then my partner asked if there had ever been someone called "Lamont" working in our fire department. It seems that the man who walked in had been looking for someone by that name that he had known long ago. He was told that no one by that name worked there.

Then it hit me; that guy had to be my old buddy, back for a visit, and he remembered me! Unfortunately, I didn't recognize him, and my partner had come on the job long after that man left the town. It bothered me that I was right there, but I still missed him, but I guess I made enough of an impression with him that he came back after all those years to visit with me. I felt good about that, but we both went away disappointed.

He Sank the Navy

I became the training officer when I was promoted to lieutenant. I made training schedules and arranged classes, but not being a senior officer, I had limited authority.

When I was promoted to captain, with the added authority came the responsibility of training the call firefighters. I love to train. My heart will always belong to the fire academy for the training I did there. I had our group at the fire station out training often. There were many things that we trained on once a year, but that's never enough.

A big thing was boat training. We only did it once a year, yet we had a lot of water with a large lake, several large ponds, and a river running through town. I know that I never felt like I was good enough with the boats back then. Besides the boats themselves, there were all the things we carried in them: ropes, ice rescue equipment, throw bags, and other things for ice or water rescue. When I could, I started to get drills scheduled for things we didn't do often.

One weekday, when there was no one at the town beach on the lake, I took the group for a boat drill. We had been running the motors and getting the feel of the boats when the motor on one of them quit and wouldn't restart. So we switched to the other boat. It didn't take long for that one to quit, too. OK, both boats were out of service, so we packed everything up and returned to quarters.

The chief was at some conference at the academy. Dispatch called him to notify him of the latest developments. I'm told he hung up his phone and announced that "Captain LeBlanc sank the navy," to which they all got a good laugh, and I got my chops busted for some time after. Command is a lonely place!

Technology Confusion

In the fire service, change comes slowly and grudgingly. We're comfortable with the way we do things, so things around the firehouse can be predictable at times. In fact, "Because that's the way we've always done it," is a pretty common thing to hear. For years, we relied on the radio and the telephone for communication...that would be *landline* telephone.

Years back, the department had a few radios to hand out to the guys. Other guys bought their own scanners and listened to the alarm of fire as it came over the radios. Then all off-duty firefighters were expected to respond to their assigned stations to man the other apparatus that stayed in quarters during that fire call.

If people are needed to cover the stations when it is not for a fire, like when the ambulance is transporting a patient to a hospital, a call was made by landline phone to get someone there. During the weekdays with off-duty firefighters away at other jobs, we would get whoever was available. At night, on weekends, and on holidays, the calls were made off of a list that was prepared at the beginning of the shift. The calls were supposed to go in order down the list so everyone had an equal chance at getting overtime.

The evolution of our station coverage list is a long, confusing story. In the beginning, no one refused any overtime. Those were the older guys who worked whenever they could. Over the years, the names and faces changed, but our means of calling people back didn't...not until it had to.

Way back, we all had our landlines. Then, I remember the first guy to get an answering machine. That guy was never home, and was one of the older guys that didn't work overtime very often, but still we had to call him when his name came up on the list. One day, the guy making the phone calls got sick of getting that answering machine and he left a message on it. I don't remember what the message was, but it wasn't nice!

The next day, we were all eating lunch. The chief was in the room, too. Then the answering machine guy came storming into the room with his answering machine in hand. He slammed it down on the table in front of the chief and was yelling something like, "I don't have to take that!" and so on. The chief told him to pick up that thing and get it the hell out of there! That's just what the guy did. The story became part of his legacy. The guy wasn't really a whirling dervish. He just had a big mouth.

The next problem to arise involved me and cell phones. The guys used to drive me crazy with those. Each man was supposed to give a phone number where he most likely could be reached. That was the number I used, but cells were showing their ugly heads and some guys were putting in two numbers. We had to cover the station and didn't have time to be dialing two numbers for people. The problem was never really addressed while I was there.

When I was a shift commander, we worked twenty-four hour shifts. One beautiful Sunday morning in July, I got a call from station 2. One of my guys told me he was going to be going home at 1800 on personal leave. That's fine, but since we were running short anyway, I was going to have to cover his slot. The rules said that I needed to wait until something like 4:30 in the afternoon to start making calls. I looked around and said to myself, "*Self,*" I said, "*If I wait until 4:30, there won't be anyone reachable on a beautiful day like this and we'll be screwed.*"

Well, since I was in charge, I made the executive decision to start calling right then. I went quite a ways through the list. There were answering machines, refusals, and no answers before I finally got someone to come in. "*Fine, I have things covered,*" I thought.

Some hours later, I got a call from another guy. He had gotten off work that morning. He told me that a man on the day shift told him he would be going home at 1800. The guy said that he knew his name was next on the coverage list and he wanted to know if the man at station 2 had called me yet. I told him that he had called me first thing that morning and I already had the shift covered. The guy became angry with me. He said he had been at church and he had gone home right after and I wasn't supposed to make any calls until 4:30. I didn't owe him any explanation, but I gave him my thoughts on what I did. He didn't like it at all, so I told him to talk to the deputy or file a grievance.

He did talk to someone and during the next officers' meeting there was one captain that began to scold me. He said I couldn't make calls before 4:30. I explained to the officers in the room my whole reason for calling early and what would have happened if I had waited. I could have, but I decided to err on the side of caution. Besides, those two guys could have let me know the facts at shift change that morning. I guess the thought of all that overtime money just clouded the mind. I said that a decision had to be made and I made it! Nothing more was ever said. Maybe I got a reprieve, or just maybe I was right!

The Phantom

Anywhere there is a career fire department, the firehouse is home. We sleep, wash, eat, cook, and clean there. Each day has someone assigned to do things like clean the kitchen or bathroom. Being a small town, station 2 always has a lot of visitors, mostly people we know. There are also many stopping by to look at the trucks or ask directions or use the bathroom. We keep things clean and it pisses us off when someone messes things up.

For years, we had someone we called the "Phantom Shitter." Try as we might, we couldn't pin it on anybody. The guy would come in when we were busy and just blast the toilet. We watched closely for years until finally we narrowed things down to a certain person who happened to be an officer on another department. He knew some of the guys at our station, and he felt free to come in, do his thing, and then leave without telling anyone. Before anyone could talk to him, we got word that he had retired and not long afterwards, he died.

Thanks for the memories, brother!

An Unwelcome Change

From time to time during my career, there would be personnel transfers to different groups, when needed. Often people need to change groups because of promotions, among other things. We had a chief for a lot of years that seemed to like to nip any problems in the bud, and changed schedules pretty often...at least it seemed that way to me.

I was put on group B when I started. Just before my probation was over, I was called into the chief's office. The deputy and my captain were there, too. It seemed that two older guys on another shift couldn't get along with each other. One guy was hard to work with because he was a slob and he smoked and the TV belonged to him, or so he acted.

The other guy was hard to work with, too. He was a well-known backstabber, who, I think, screwed everyone he'd ever known. Well, he stabbed his partner in the back and made up stories about him.

Things were heating up, so they took the easiest solution they could think of: put the new kid with Mr. Backstabber. They asked me if I saw any problem with that. What could I say? My probation wasn't over quite yet, so what I said didn't matter. I was transferred to that other group to work with him at station 2.

When I walked out of the meeting where I was told of my new schedule, my captain took me aside and told me, hinting at what my new partner might do, "Watch your ass. Other people might give you a hard time, but they won't fuck you." That put me on edge, but the partnership was fine–for a while.

As soon as I stopped agreeing with everything he said, he stopped being nice. Understand, I was still a new guy and didn't want to mouth off too much. He made my life a living hell for two and a half years. I almost left the fire service, that's what kind of a guy my partner was. Many others felt the same way about him, but I had to live with him.

When I couldn't stand it any longer, I made an appointment to see the chief on a day off and told him my tale. This was a different chief than the one who sent me to that group. That chief had retired and this new one knew very well about the problems I had with my partner. He agreed to get me transferred. I explained to my partner that things weren't working out and I was transferred over to station 1, but still on the same shift. That was good. No new guy should be sent to work with Mr. Backstabber.

There were other shake ups with the scheduling, too. I guess the chief thought it needed to be done. Damned if I know why. I stayed where I was for a couple of years until there was another shake up and I was put on another group. I ended up working on that group for the next twenty plus years. I was the only one from my group who got transferred.

I was put at headquarters with a couple of guys I knew, but they came on the job after me. The man I replaced on that group was an older guy. The other guys on the group liked him and they resented the shake up. From the beginning, I wasn't feeling welcome at all. There were a lot of secret conversations. As a small department, it's tough not to have any contact with someone while in the firehouse, but they tried.

The two guys I worked with on that group were the only two people who came on after me during some major budget problems. As a result, neither of them ever went to any academy or got any other formal training. On the job training isn't a good idea for probies. They can only get as good as the guy who teaches them, and if that guy is a couch potato, they'll learn next to nothing.

There was a new guy I worked with when I was on an overtime shift on his group, the group that I was later transferred to. He was on one of his first shifts. He was kind of a know-it-all. He was also overweight and lazy. He once told me that he didn't like to be hot, tired, or dirty...great career choice. We were doing some mundane chore or another, and two of the new guys started to ask about street locations.

This guy looked up at us and said, "If this is a drill, I don't want to play!"

Wow, and from a probie, no less.

By the time I was put on that group, the guy was through his probation, but was no less lazy. He didn't like to admit that he might not know something. He would wait until he was alone and no one could see him looking up the information.

One day, he and the other guy on our shift walked across the apparatus floor and the big guy was carrying a book. The other guy was still kind of new, very tall, and thin, and not a bad guy at all. I could have worked well with just him and I, but he seemed to be under the influence of the big guy and wasn't overly friendly to me. They walked over to the boat and got out a piece of rope. The book told them how to tie knots, and they were trying to learn to tie a bowline. I had spent some time working in the tree business and the bowline is a basic knot in that business. They were having some problems, so I stepped up, got a piece of rope, and proceeded to show them how to tie the knot. I was trying to help and I was not showing off, but they looked disgusted with me, put the rope away, and walked away. OK with me. That big guy was tough to work with. He didn't want to be shown anything–especially by me.

Another time, we had gotten a new saw and the captain called us together to learn to use it. The big guy was absent. He took the owner's manual and went off by himself. We all had a turn starting and running the saw. Then we put it away. No one ever said anything about that guy not being with us during the training.

A little while later, I heard a noise coming from the back room shop area. It was the sound of a small motor that someone was trying to start. Also present was the strong smell of gasoline.

I walked out back and there he was, pulling away at the starter cord. The manual choke was wide open, and it was so flooded that gas was all over the saw. Now, I know that not everybody has a lot of experience with small motors and manual chokes. I have a lot of experience and tried to help him by telling him to close the choke. I knew it wasn't going to start the way he was doing it.

He looked at me and said, "The manual said to use the choke on a cold engine. It doesn't say to use it when *Lewie LeBlanc* says so." He put the saw away and never got it started.

I guess I shouldn't have been surprised. I worked with that man for some years until he was transferred to another shift. I had problems with him from the beginning. After he left the group, things got better, but I still never felt like one of the group.

Look Before You Leap

I remember well one day at station 1. We had a full shift: me, two other guys, plus the captain. As I remember, it was afternoon, shortly after lunch, and the guys and I were talking in the day room, when the captain walked through with his shaving bag and went into the bathroom. A few minutes later, the captain stuck his head out and asked if anyone had any toothpaste. One of the guys got up, went to his locker, and grabbed a tube. Walking into the day room, he tossed the tube to the captain, who grabbed it and closed the door.

We were talking again when the bathroom door opened, and in the doorway stood the captain. He had white foamy stuff all around his mouth and a mortified look on his face. His hand held a toothbrush all covered with the same white foamy stuff.

The captain just looked at us and said, "It's shave cream!"

He cleaned himself up and we looked at the tube. Sure as hell, it was indeed shave cream in a tube. I can't believe anyone would do that on purpose. But, as the saying goes, "Shit happens." Maybe he should have looked at the label.

A Sight to Be Remembered

The town I worked for was a relatively small one, and the fire department was only one generation away from its roots as an all-call department. The part of town where I lived was kind of thickly settled. Everyone knew each other and there were some real characters. This story is true; I was there.

Back when I was a kid, I lived next door to two brothers. They were about a year apart with the older one being my age and the other about a year or two younger. The older one was a thin, wiry kid, and his brother was a bit chubby. Their mother was a single parent back before it became fashionable, and she was quite a tough, rugged-looking woman. The two boys were a couple of wild men, even when we were young. Still, they were the first friends I can remember having.

I think I was about ten or twelve when the younger boy had his mishap. Like many kids then, he had a stingray bicycle with the high rise handlebars and a banana seat. We all had bicycles and used and abused them every day. Well, this kid had a problem with the bike seat. It kept coming detached from the seat post and it would rock backward on its support rods. To cure this, the kid's answer was to stand up on the pedals and sit down hard to push the seat back down. I guess it must have worked in the short term, because he kept on doing it.

One day, while riding in the ballpark across the street, the seat popped off the post, and unbeknownst to him, it rocked way back, more than usual. He stood up on the pedals and sat down—hard. As he came down, he never realized that there was no seat under him. He sat down on the seat post. The post entered his body, but did not use the existing entrance; it made a whole new one.

As he lay there screaming and impaled on his bike, someone went and got his mother. She came over, and ever the Amazon, she put her foot on the kid and wrenched the bike off–and out–of him. She then got him home and drove him to the hospital.

The kid healed up OK. He had to wear a bag for a while as his insides healed. To this day I can still see his mother pulling that bike out. It still makes me cringe!

Eeewwwwww!

In the course of my life and certainly my work, I have seen things that I wish I could forget, and worked places where I would have loved not to be. Somehow, I'm able to just do what has to be done and remain detached from it. I have some bad memories, though. There are also a few things that people do that I find positively disgusting.

I was repulsed when a guy I worked with would sit in the day room and brush his teeth. He could have used the bathroom, but he didn't, and brushed away for all to see. Sure, I could have gotten up and left the room, which is what I did, but what the hell. I thought it was gross and bad manners. Then, on top of that, he'd leave his toothbrush on the table or the back of a chair and forget about it. If I saw it there, I used to get a wad of paper towels, pick up the brush, and throw it in the dumpster out back. I don't know how many toothbrushes I threw away, or what the guy thought was happening to his toothbrushes, but I can tell you, I did discard quite a few.

When I was very new, or perhaps a call firefighter still, I heard a story about a couple of older guys on the department. One guy had false teeth, or perhaps I should say that he had *some* false teeth. He only had an upper plate. I heard that sometime before, the guy had thrown up in a toilet and lost his lower plate there. I guess he decided against retrieving it. So really, as long as I knew him, he only had top teeth.

The other guy also had false teeth, but still had both plates. Now, I don't remember what the occasion was, but there were a bunch of guys at the firehouse talking. The guy with only top teeth was feeling something wrong with his plate; it didn't feel right. He took it out and looked at it. Then he looked at the guy sitting next to him, the guy with both plates. That guy looked back, took out his upper plate, handed it to the other guy, and took his. They both slipped the false teeth into their mouths and smiled. They had each had the other one's false teeth, and swapped like it was perfectly natural. I still get queasy when I think of that. I've seen many things much worse, but that dental plate story is just gross!

Keys

Firefighters are on duty twenty-four hours a day because shit happens at night, too, as well as weekends and holidays. When things happen in commercial buildings when no one is working, we are often required to gain entry to find and correct the problem. Getting into someplace is easy, even easier if one doesn't care what one breaks. Business owners don't like to have things broken. We could call the owner, or designated person, to let us in every time there is a problem, but that doesn't always work. People are away or there's a big storm and we have to break in, anyway.

At some point, someone had the idea to get keys from the establishment owners who were willing, tag them, secure them in a key box, and carry them in the duty officer's car. I think most places gave us a key, and things worked well for a while.

We also had some bed-ridden residents in town who gave us keys to their homes. That way, if they had a problem, we could get in to help.

Then, with lots of new construction, that increased the number of businesses dramatically. Before too long, the key box was past full. Those boxes aren't made to be carried around. They are the type that usually gets mounted on a wall. That works well for most purposes, but we needed those keys with us. I imagine that there was something made that could have filled our needs, but as far as I know, no one ever looked for it. That key box was a pain in the ass. Then, when it dropped and keys spilled all over the ground, that was enough to really piss someone off.

That key box was with us until the coming of the lock box. A lock box could be securely installed on the outside wall of the building. We would keep that building's key in their lock box, so all we needed to carry was one master key for the lock box itself. We'd open that and get their key.

The town grew and the population changed to have more professional people in higher-end homes with alarm systems that sounded when the people were not home. These people started to get lock boxes for their homes, too. Oh sure, we still had those lockout calls and well-being checks that often required us to break in, but they became fewer over a short time.

Those lock boxes were a great idea, the kind of idea that people shake their heads and say, "Why didn't I think of that?"

Uniforms

It wasn't too long before I came on the job that the guys were wearing dungarees and denim jackets. By the time I arrived, there was a uniform consisting of dark blue shirts, (short sleeved for summer and long for winter), dark blue work pants, black shoes, and a black belt. If you wore a hat, it had to be the firefighter's bell cap. The department also issued your first class A uniform, although we were expected to keep it up for our career if it needed any changes. As us young guys got older and fatter, sometimes alterations or replacements were required. Also, when promotions came, some parts of the class A uniform were different with the new rank, so they had to be replaced: the dress coat had to be double breasted, a white bell cap was needed, and a braid was added to the hat.

When I got hired, the department clerk ordered me some uniforms and bought me some shoes from a salesman who used to come around every couple of weeks. Back then, for some reason, all the guys I worked with wore shoes and not boots like years later. Well, the shoes sucked and the pants didn't fit right and were of poor quality, so the pockets ripped out and the material pilled and lost its shape. Other than that, everything was fine.

When I walked in my first day of work, there was a move afoot to change the uniform to light blue shirts. The chief said that if we all agreed, we could change it. So there were several different styles hanging in the day room for us to look at. One was chosen and the new uniform shirt would start to be worn at uniform change in May when we switched back from long sleeved shirts to short sleeved shirts.

Well, it was around September and I had to buy long sleeve, dark blue shirts to wear for my first winter. We got a clothing allowance. It wasn't too much and I still had to buy my light blue, short sleeved shirts for spring. Cost me a little money out-of-pocket, but what the hell. Ya gotta do what ya gotta do.

The shirts remained the same for years, but the pants became a problem again. Everyone had pretty much stopped buying those crappy ones because a couple of other brands were available. They had to be dark blue with a flat front—no pleats. We did have a guy that either didn't know or didn't care about that and spent his clothing allowance on pleated pants. Holy hell was raised by the boss.

This brought attention to another problem with the pants: not all navy blue pants are the same shade of blue. Some looked very different from others. No one had really paid attention until the Great Pleated Pants Caper. Now the chief put the pants issue under a microscope.

I was a captain by this time, and I told the boss that I found a place to buy navy blue pants, the right shade, for dirt cheap. I had been wearing them for years. The chief looked around and settled on uniform pants from somewhere else that cost about two and a half times what I had been paying. The chief designated those pants to be the required uniform pants. Guess what? They pilled and lost their shape! Come full circle!

But I never bought any of those expensive pants. Mine were the right shade of blue. If the boss wanted to check the tag, he'd have to pants me and that wasn't going to happen!

What we wore as a winter coat was up to us. Many people wore that kind of quilted coat that we all had. They even had lined ones for cold weather. I wore that and I was fine, but I guess they were looking for a good cold weather coat. Samples were brought in and a coat was chosen that we all had to buy with clothing allowance or out-of-pocket money. I got that coat and wore it that winter and it was nice. After that one winter, those coats disappeared and there was no word of them again. Don't know what happened. I guess the chief forgot about it!

Then, after many years of light blue, the guys wanted to change to dark blue shirts. This new batch of guys didn't like cleaning light blue work shirts. I guess the dark blue ones hide stains better. They're hotter in the summer, but that's what they wanted. Me? I was a captain by then and wearing white shirts.

On our department, the officers wore badges. I was always happy not to wear one; it could get caught on things. But the guys wanted badges. The chief decided and they were told that they will wear them as part of the uniform every time they came to work. I had to wear it, so I did. Not too long after that, I had to send one of my guys home to get his badge. He forgot it. But rules are rules.

Had It Been Another Day

The state firefighting academy has had a great many programs to offer, and through the years there have been a few that just kind of disappeared. A big problem is that the wheels of government move slowly, and there is often no money in a certain budget to buy or replace needed equipment and props. Admittedly, things wear out and vehicles rust, but if one washes the vehicle each time it's used, and practiced better maintenance, more time could be gotten out of things.

Years back, the academy had two travel trailers all decked out to look like a kitchen inside and fitted with a sprinkler head. While people observed, a small fire was lit in a wastebasket under the sprinkler. Sure enough, the sprinkler head would open, water would spray, and the fire would be put out. This program showed what a home sprinkler system could do.

These two trailers went out often and were towed by a pickup truck. Two people operated the props in the trailer, while the instructor talked to the class. It was a popular class, but after a time, the trailers were wearing out. One was in too bad a shape to be used anymore. That left just the other one.

One summer morning, two men were going to be leaving from the academy with a pickup towing that trailer. The man who would be the passenger was a well-thought-of worker. He also had a well-known drinking problem. He was a firefighter in a nearby town. I knew him well and I can say, without a doubt, that there were people who never knew the man drank because they never had seen him sober. That problem didn't slow him down at all for a lot of years. He was a guy you wanted around when there was work to be done, until the alcohol finally got the best of him, and then he'd forget to come to work. He lost his job at the fire department.

On the day they were towing the trailer, the guy was doing alright. The second man, the one who would be driving, was part-time help for the summer. He wasn't a firefighter, but he was the son of the director of the academy.

They left with the trailer and got on the highway. They were tooling along pretty well when a semi passed them in the next lane, moving along fast. The draft from that semi pulled the trailer out sideways, where it disintegrated all over the highway. They called to report what happened and the academy sent another truck, this time a bigger, rack body truck, and some help to pick up the remains. They got the bits and pieces of that trailer onto the rack body and took it back to the academy. The thing looked a lot smaller than when it had left earlier.

The people in administration at the academy have a tendency to find fault with people and use that as an excuse to fire them. Funny though, nothing more was ever said about this incident. I have to wonder...what if the other guy had been driving?

The White Wave of Death

Years ago, I lived pretty near a farm. There were many different animals there. We saw everything from baby pigs to sheep...which, oddly enough, is the subject of my story.

One day, a lady friend and I took my kids to the farm. They were small then. They liked to look at the animals. I should say that this lady friend of mine had a deep seated fear of sheep. I think it stemmed from a long ago incident involving being waylaid by a flock of sheep and bullied and abused. The memory of that incident still lingers today.

Well, as we walked around the outside of the barn to see the cows, we passed the sheep enclosure, which was quite full. When we were done, there was only one way for us to get back: the way we came, past those sheep. We hadn't made it to the sheep pen yet when my lady friend broke into a run in the direction of the pen. Then as she cut to the left to get around the side of the barn again, I looked and saw the sheep charging the fence. Just as she got around the barn, the fence came down. There were sheep wandering everywhere, with me laughing like a fool during this attack by the killer sheep. I think I might have found her up on top of something that the sheep, lacking an opposable thumb, couldn't climb. Maybe I'm just being cruel...but I think it's funny!

[Note from the editor (aka the "lady friend"): The sheep all ganged up and tried to get me. It was terrifying!]

Tools of the Trade

Every day that I went to work, I found someone who thought they knew my job better than me. People have a lot of things to say when we do things like take an engine to the store to shop for a meal to cook. If the place is close, sometimes a guy will walk over to it with a portable radio in his pocket. Other times, someone will take one of the smaller vehicles to shop, taking a portable radio into the store. If a call comes in, the guys shopping either get back to the firehouse fast or respond right to the incident from there.

I've heard people criticize firefighters for doing that. They don't understand that there might be a place close by to shop where the firefighter can go on the engine, shop as fast as they can, and return to quarters as soon as possible. Sometimes the engine company might already be out doing inspections or returning from a call. On the way back to the station, they stop and pick up food. The firefighters live together and eat together at the firehouse. Often meals are cooked in-house...so you have to shop.

Another thing people do is tell us how to respond and what vehicles to take to the call. Years ago, when I was dispatching, I'd get calls from people telling me not to send a fire engine or not to use the lights or siren. Maybe they think we use those things for fun. The fact is that the fire engine is a tool, as is each thing on that engine. We never know what's going to happen, so we take our tools with us to a call. Everything on that engine is something we might have to use. One never calls a plumber, electrician, or carpenter and tells them what tools to bring. He drives a truck to go to jobs and the vehicle has the things that those folks use to do their jobs. So when you see a fire engine on the road or parked someplace, they're not wasting time or money, and they have their tools with them!

Ahhhhh, the Chiefs...

I think every firefighter has opinions of their chief. It's interesting to look back at them and see how different they were from each other.

I worked for four different chiefs and have an abundance of stories about each one of them. The first was an old World War 2 veteran coming to the end of his fire service career and just wanted a chief's job somewhere to boost his retirement pension. The place he came from was much bigger and busier than our department, and this guy was just out of his element. He wasn't around long...he retired as soon as he could.

The next guy in the door was the first deputy chief the department had. He had worked himself up through the ranks and eventually became chief. He had even grown up in town. I say that he was the best chief I worked for. Others may disagree, but that's my opinion.

He was a long time member of the department and there had been many changes through the years. This chief often became involved in more personal issues with the other guys. There was a lot of bad blood between him and other long time members of the department, some of it because they wouldn't take any shit lying down. For a while, the boss couldn't make a move without someone from the group jumping on him and starting a whole new problem. As a result, he resorted to revenge after the muckrakers in the department continued to cause trouble.

When I first came on the fire department, if you were scheduled to work on Thanksgiving or Christmas, you could not put in for having one of those days off. No vacation would be granted. That was the rule, until one of the guys decided to put in for Christmas. There was a big problem and it ended with us running a man short. That would be fine...unless a second person requested vacation also. His position would have to be covered with somebody on overtime. That sounds great in theory, but who the hell wants to work the holiday?

There were some young single guys who often would cover for the guys with kids, but you couldn't always get one of them to work. If the vacation could not be filled, then the chief could refuse the vacation and the guy would have to arrange to swap shifts with someone or work it himself.

Then came the Christmas when two people had put in for vacation. The second slot couldn't be filled and the chief posted a memo saying that if no one would volunteer to work, we would run short by two men. The union president should have fought this, but he was having his own problems with the chief. He claimed that his position as fire alarm superintendent was being threatened. Instead of addressing the vacation issue as union president, he was only interested in his own position. I remember tearing into him when I saw him next for putting a personal problem before the welfare of the guys.

I don't think anyone thought that the chief would actually let two guys be out on Christmas, but sure enough, on Christmas morning, I went to work at station 2 to find we were short by two people, just as the boss had said. The chief also shirked his duty to the people of the town, all in the name of revenge. By having us run short two men, he potentially endangered everybody on duty.

The next chief came when the fire department, as I knew it, started to come apart. A lot of the time the chief was who-knows-where. All the stuff we came to expect as part of our jobs was forgotten: no more inspecting the tools, no more refinishing wooden handles, no more inspecting ladders, etc. We used to color-code our tools to show which engine they belonged to, but now color-coding was forgotten. Hell, we didn't even test hose for a couple of years! Oh sure, there were guys who did those things on their own, but when it wasn't done, no one said anything.

There was no money for anything, either. I don't know how he presented a budget each year, and I don't know what he did with the money, but there was money for nothing at all, except at the extremes of circumstances. Nothing, but the smallest amounts, was spent on gear and tools. It was then that the yearly medical physicals that were once required went the way of the buffalo.

He kept a mattress in his office hallway so when we had a big snow storm or other malady, instead of calling in extra men, he would stay at the firehouse. He never went out on any calls, so he was pretty much useless. He would have been just as useless if he had gone out with us, so we didn't press things. No ex-extra help, but we did have an extra man in the firehouse!

He used to go out shopping and come back with new things. A couple of times he came back with Gateway computers in his car. Why or where he got those, who knows.

He once went to a convention of some sort and came back with two airpacks of a brand that we'd never heard of. We always used Scotts. These were something like ISI. They were totally different from that which we were used to using. No one was trained on them, but he said that they were to be placed on the apparatus. They were, but no one ever grabbed one.

Once I told him about a piece of equipment a friend told me about. It was something to clamp over the steering wheel of a car during extrication to protect us if the air bag inflated suddenly. I said that it sounded worth investigating. A few days later I asked him if he had a chance to take a look at the tool. I was curious.

He said, "I bought one!"

Oh great, Santa Claus strikes again. I just wanted to look at one.

Well, we got one. We looked it over and tried it out on a junk car. It was a steel plate with sharp points designed to deflate a deploying airbag. It was cool, in theory, but while affixing this thing to the steering wheel, there was every chance of an air bag suddenly deploying, sending it flying, which would injure or kill a rescuer. We told our officer about this, but the chief ordered that this tool be carried on the apparatus and drilled with. On it went and it came out to drill with, but eventually that stopped. We were never going to use it anyway!

We were always trying to get abandoned houses slated for demolition to use for training purposes, especially when I became training officer. I loved to train like that...realistic, even if we didn't get to light it on fire. There are many other jobs to be done at a fire, not just putting out the fire, so we could practice on lots of other things.

The chief found a house just up the street from where I lived that we might be able to use. He was talking about using it for live fire training. Trouble was, the place was covered with old asbestos siding. That stuff is nothing to fool around with, and you need to have a team of specialists to remove it.

The boss, of course, had a plan. He would ask for volunteers and spring for a couple of cold platters and a few six packs and the vollies would take their hammers to the siding, sending asbestos all over the neighborhood, then bag it and sneak it into the town landfill. I never voiced my concerns to the boss, but if he had gone through with scheduling that job, I was going to call the EPA and put a stop to it. I didn't have to, in the end. He had an acute lack of volunteers and so the job was forgotten.

Back room politics and wheeling and dealing were how he did things. I don't think the guy meant to be dishonest. He just thought that things were done that way.

I could go on and on about this chief, but I'll say just one more thing about him. He had back bone. I was having trouble with schools wedging open some fire doors and chaining others open. It was against the fire safety laws and I wrote a report. I returned a few days later and found the same thing; nothing had changed.

I went back and told the chief. He jumped into his car and told me to follow him back to the school. There, he told me to get the bolt cutters and remove the chains from the walls and door stops from the hall doors, while he went into the office and proceeded tell them the facts of life as far as fire safety went. They looked dumbstruck as we left.

The problem would return with the next chief. I was told that the next chief told the schools that they could block the doors open, so they did. State law said no, but the chief said it was OK.

This new chief was from a nearby town that was even smaller than ours. He was an arrogant little guy who loved to be in the spot light. He loved being chief, but he wouldn't sit at the kitchen table to have coffee with the guys unless there was an officer there. Took him less than six months to alienate the whole department. No one had anything nice to say about this guy. They started calling him "Coin Toss" due to his frequent changes of plans. He could, however, write a grant and did get some great things for the department, but he was just a jerk and I was glad to retire. I'd had enough.

One in Ten Thousand

I remember when I first got into the fire service. We didn't even think of wearing gloves, and we still did mouth to mouth resuscitation on strangers. There wasn't so much disposable equipment...some was cleaned and used again.

Then HIV/AIDS showed its ugly head and the scramble was on for protection. The fire department got some disposable gloves for the ambulance and engine. It was around this time that the deputy was asking us not to use them unless necessary. I told him that as far as I was concerned, I was going to wear them on every call.

When the deputy started buying gloves for the ambulance, he had just assumed that the men would wear large or XL, so that was all he bought. Then I asked him to buy some for my size hands: medium. Who the hell can work if there's a half inch of glove hanging from the end of your fingers? The way the deputy carried on, you'd think that he'd paid for them himself! But that all died down and it was common for me to wear two pairs of gloves or more—one of a few new habits to be developed to avoid disease.

The next big disease to affect us was hepatitis B. This was such a serious threat that it was mandated that we all get inoculated against it. The vaccine was given on duty and there were three shots, as I remember. It escapes me how long we waited between shots, but it was not very long at all. A short time after the third shot, we took a test—they called it a titer test—to see if we had developed the antibodies. Well, my titer came back negative: no antibodies. They gave me a booster and a titer shortly after. Still no antibodies, so they did it again: booster, then a titer. When the third titer came back negative, they got the hint. They told me to "Glove up!" Great idea! I found out that only one in ten thousand people fail to develop antibodies. Maybe I wasn't lucky, but I was unique among ten thousand people!

I was working per diem with an ambulance company not too long after. I worked shifts with many different people, but after a while I met a guy who, like me, was an off-duty firefighter making a buck on the side. We really hit it off well and tried to schedule shifts together. It wasn't hard as he worked for another town, but worked the exact same schedule as I did. We became friends and are still friends today. In one of the many conversations in the ambulance, we were talking about our departments and the subject of hep B shots came up. I told him how things had gone for me and how I didn't make antibodies.

He looked at me and said, "Me neither."

Hmmmmm...one in ten thousand people. Well, now there were two of us together. He wasn't lucky either and I wasn't unique anymore!

What the Hell Was That?

There was a guy I worked with years back who lived in an apartment right near the firehouse. Outside of work, I never spent much time with him. We just didn't connect, but we got along, and that was good as we had to work together. Some years, the group would meet at his apartment and go out for a shift dinner at Christmas time.

One evening, I went to his place for some kind of gathering or another. I walked in and something buzzed me. Something was flying around the apartment. I ducked–to the amusement of those already there. The guy had a pet bird that I didn't know about. It was a small bird and he let it fly free in the apartment. It was cute and friendly and fun to watch. It would even land on us and sit there on your finger.

Then our shift commander showed up. He walked in and the bird flew to him.

He jumped and said, "What the hell was that?"

We started to laugh...until he began to swat at the thing flying around. He didn't hit the bird, but we left for our function soon after and probably saved the poor little bird from getting squashed.

The Bus

One day, when I was a very new guy on the fire department, I was loafing on a day off when one of the guys on the department tracked me down and asked me to help out. The new guy always gets asked. Turns out that the academy in the early days had a public education bus. They would take it to schools and teach the children. Inside were bells and alarms that the kids could make work and learn how to report a fire. There was a fire alarm box in there, all set up to be tripped, and we could open it so the kids could watch what happens when you trip a box.

I had a cute little girl, probably about four or five, come up to the box with her bright eyes shining and a big smile on her face. She was looking at the box and I asked her if she knew what was in there. She smiled and said softly that there was a little man in there that got the signal and made the box work.

Just thinking of her as she said that, smiling, so sure she was right, makes me smile after all these years. She wasn't disappointed when I showed her what was actually inside the box. She looked interested and listened and thanked me when she was done. That was among the cutest things that I have ever seen.

Just Do Your Job

With any job I ever had, I never had my eye on a boss's position. That's not to say I never wanted to be promoted, but I listened, watched, and did my job. That made me popular with some of the program coordinators at the academy. Though I worked mostly with the recruits, there was a coordinator who used to ask me to teach new staff members to use the burn building. The whole building is a tool, in and of itself, to teach firefighting. There were many things we could do with it, and different scenarios we could create. Even before I was an officially certified instructor, he had me teaching new instructors.

One day, I was scheduled to work, but as I was coming off duty at the fire station, I was late. There was another guy there who was loud and bragging, and really wanted to be in charge inside the burn building. He was standing around getting ready to play the big shot when I came walking up. His face dropped when the coordinator came out and welcomed me warmly, and then explained to *me* what he wanted done. I chuckled under my breath. Maybe if the other guy would shut up, someone would take a better look at him. Being well thought of is a good thing. All you have to do is to know your job and do it with no argument.

Another day, that same coordinator came to me with an offer. He said that there was a television crew coming in to shoot a scene for the National Fire Protection Association. He needed people to keep a fire going at the windows of the second floor of the burn building. We would not be in the shoot; we just had to keep the fire going. He said that it might run very late. He asked me if I would be interested in working.

I answered, "Yes," and then he asked me how many people we'd need for the job. I said that four of us should be enough. He said that was fine and told me to pick my crew. Wow! Pick *my* crew! I guess that meant I was supposed to be boss. First thing I did was ask three people that needed no boss. Good workers all, and we made the whole academy look good! Everything went off very well, and it was very interesting working with a real film crew with a director and everything, plus they fed us well!

I got home about 0230, tired as hell, but it had been a great time. Reputation is worth a lot, and if you have a good one, you get the good stuff!

Wow...Just Wow...

This story happened in a town near mine. It was told to me by a friend who was there as the captain of a rescue company that arrived on scene. I don't remember how they received the call, but it was in an upscale neighborhood, full of professional people who made a lot of money.

My friend told me that when they pulled up, there was something on the lawn, something that shouldn't be there. It proved to be the heart and lungs of the woman of the house, impaled on sticks in the front yard.

The original story said that she had burned the ziti and the husband got pissed off. There have been alterations to the story of exactly what happened, but it did involve ziti and the murder was real. I never found out any more about this incident, but the story is true as far as I have told it. You just don't know what people are capable of.

Robots

The state firefighting academy site is the home of the state fire marshal and the other offices that answer to the marshal. The state police bomb squad also operates out of there.

One day, when working at the academy, I noticed something going on in the gas school. There was no gas class. When I walked over, I found a meeting of the bomb squads from around New England, and they had brought their robots. The troopers were operating and practicing with the robots. They also tried out each other's machines. It was fun watching them. I never would have thought there would be so many different models. Looking at them, I was brought back to the scene in Star Wars when Luke and his uncle went to the dealer to get a couple of new droids.

Those guys all seemed to be proud of their robots! I wonder which one works best.

Police Matter

Sometimes we get dispatched to a residence for a well-being check to make sure the resident is OK. It used to be that the police would respond, too, and they often got there first.

One night, a call came in for a man who couldn't be awakened. The police responded first. Our south side engine responded, too, but got there after the police. When they arrived, the police cruiser was sitting in the street in front of the house with the officer inside his car. He was waiting for the fire department. He didn't want to go in until we got there.

Well, he went in with the engine company and found the patient in full arrest. The cop left and the firefighters called for the ambulance and went to work starting CPR. The ambulance got there, and the patient was transported with CPR in progress. I have to think that the cop wasted precious time by sitting in his car waiting for us to show up. That cop did exactly what I expected him to do: sat in his cruiser until somebody else came to do the work. So after that, the fire department sent a full response to every well-being check and didn't depend on the police.

Most cops are pretty good, but the one who was there on the night in question was bottom of the barrel. He worked night shifts so he could sleep on duty. Then he'd get lucrative overtime pay working road details during the day.

There were a couple of others on the night shifts that weren't what one would expect of a police officer. One of them would drive around looking for problems and he'd call for the ambulance for trivial things. We got pissed off, but I guess that's what we're here for.

Often, when we got calls for checks on people who hadn't been seen for a few days, it didn't end well. We usually had to break in and look around. If we found a body, it was usually a day or two old—and fragrant. We'd check the patient, and if we determined that the patient was workable, then we'd start CPR and get the defibrillator and oxygen. Often, though, it was too late because the patient had been down too long.

One morning in the summer, I was commanding the shift for the day. I was in car 2 at station 2 when the call came in for a well-being check just about a minute away from the firehouse. The engine was dispatched from station 2, and the ambulance was dispatched from station 1, about three miles away. I got there in the car at the same time as the engine. On that engine were very experienced men. They started to look into windows to see if they could see anyone. On well-being checks we always look for easy ways to gain entry, perhaps through an unlocked door or window. That's always better than having to force our way in. Sure enough, one of my guys came around the house and said he saw a man on the floor in the open bathroom doorway. They looked at me and asked what my orders were.

I answered simply, "Get in."

A window was broken out and a firefighter went in and unlocked the door so the rest of us could get in. The whole atmosphere suggested that this man was dead. The smell was terrible. They checked out the patient and found that he was starting to show signs of rigor mortis. It was too late for him. So I called in to dispatch that it was a "police matter," and told them to return the ambulance which had not even arrived yet. The police came in and took over.

I went back to station 1 where I got an earful from one of the newer guys on the ambulance. He had never been to a call like that before and wanted to see how things were done. I told him that we don't tie up the ambulance for a DOA. Plus, the stink was sickening. He didn't care.

That happened twenty years ago and I still get harassed by him for depriving him of a training opportunity. I think he might understand now, all these years later.

A Better Way

Change comes hard in the fire service, but it *does* come. Sometimes it comes in the form of a new piece of equipment or a change in laws. Maybe some new ideas take root and things change. It stinks when you have what you think is a good idea and no one else likes it. It can be frustrating. I remember asking about doing some things differently over the years and was shot down. The only reason given was that "We've always done it this way." I always felt that no one really gave a shit what I thought, so I just did my job and didn't make too many suggestions.

One day, it occurred to me that there was a change that we could make to make things more efficient, the way they teach it to the recruits at the academy. I brought up the idea at an officers' meeting. Without getting into the details, it had to do with deployment of a particular hose. It was all basic stuff that anyone who is a firefighter should know.

I presented my idea and was appalled to find that no one else in the room knew what I was talking about. Well, there was one guy who understood—and he disapproved because it wasn't his idea. He made some absurd statement about how those changes would affect water supply. Everyone I ever told that story to asked what the hell that guy was talking about. It was a stupid argument. He had presented it at that meeting to two other captains, one deputy, and four lieutenants, all of whom agreed with him because they didn't understand the basic principles of hydraulics. I was very much a short timer at that time, and I decided it wasn't worth an argument with a room full of people who didn't understand and didn't want to. So, the idea was dropped and we kept doing things the way we always had.

One day, fourteen years after I had retired, I got a phone call from a guy from the fire department. He had been one of my call firefighters and I had been impressed with him when he had worked for me. He was appointed to full-time shortly after I retired and had since made lieutenant. He said that he and a few others were working on some changes to the way some of the hose was packed on the engines to be deployed. He said that someone, a guy who had been a junior officer at the meeting where I had made my original proposal, mentioned my idea from years before. He asked me to explain it to him. I did and he liked it. He called me back later and told me that they had used my idea...with a necessary change or two, but *my* idea!

Imagine that, all these years later and they use my idea! Maybe we just have professional firefighters on the job, people that understand the basics, and maybe, just maybe, my idea was a better way to do it all along.

The Passenger

For a while when I was working for an ambulance company, the training division gave me jobs training staff at nursing homes and other medical facilities in the fine art of first aid and CPR. Often, when I was given a class to teach, I went in my own car and I always brought with me a full-sized adult CPR manikin. It was heavy, but I would enter the classroom with the manikin over my shoulder in a kind of fireman's carry. I got some funny looks, especially because I would sometimes be scolding the manikin as I walked in the classroom. On my drive to or from my classes, I would put it in my car in the passenger seat and fasten the seat belt. I never got stopped, but I sure did get lots of stares! It must have been a sight!

Got Him

I had two guys on my shift that didn't like each other. One was my partner when I was at station 2. Station 2 was a two-man house, so it was nice to get along with your partner. This man was a socially ignorant man, but not a bad person. It was very tough working with him with his living habits. He smoked and he even came to work tipsy at night a little too often. The guy was kind of lazy, but then again, he was as old as my parents. Maybe he thought he'd done his share of his life's work and wasn't going to do anything he didn't have to.

The other guy was the shift commander, the deputy. He'd been around since before the fire department went full-time. He'd been a call firefighter since he was old enough, and though he sounded like some old hay seed from the farm, he knew his way around a fire ground. I had known the deputy since I was a kid, having known his kids from elementary school. He'd been a captain as long as I'd known him, and he became the second deputy the department ever had. There was one thing the deputy wasn't: lazy. He was always doing something or talking to someone about the town politics. He had no use for laziness and couldn't stand that other guy at all.

The first guy couldn't wear an airpack. I don't know why, except that he said that he just couldn't breathe wearing one, so he didn't wear one. There were no rules on the department requiring us to wear SCBAs back then. We didn't carry enough for everybody and the new guys wouldn't always use one so that they could show that they could "take it." The deputy swore many times that before he retired, he was going to *make* the other guy put on an airpack.

Early one morning, just after sunrise, we got a call for a mattress fire at an address on the north end of town. I was working with my usual partner at station 2 about four miles away. Mattress fires at that hour of the day just might turn bad. Under the best of conditions, mattresses make tons of thick, black, smelly smoke. An engine was already there when we arrived and the deputy was waiting for us outside. Things were under control before we arrived, but due to the amount of smoke, the deputy kept us coming. We didn't need a hydrant, so I pulled the engine right into the driveway behind the engine that was already there. I set the brake and got out, and saw the deputy waiting. He walked right up to my partner and yelled in his face, "SCOTT AIRPACK!"

I went inside to find things under control. The other company had put the fire out and got the mattress out of the window and were wetting it down outside. There was no more smoke as my partner came into the room...

with no face piece on...

and his Scott airpack on upside down.

The deputy had fulfilled his promise—he got the guy to wear an airpack!

Couldn't Be Me

I was raised in a dysfunctional household. There were very few compliments given and not much approval, but there was lots of criticism, so I grew up with low self-esteem and less self confidence. As I got older, I concentrated on doing what was expected of me with no questions or arguments. That way, I didn't draw criticism and I got left alone. That is, until I entered the fire service. There, as the new guy, I got eaten alive.

As things went along through the years, I got better and more self-assured in what I was doing. I still got my balls busted, but then, so did everyone else. I went to work at the state fire academy and met people from all over the state. Once I got acclimated, things went well for me there, too. But I still lacked the confidence to take any lead position. I didn't feel that there was anything I could tell anybody that they needed to hear.

I should mention here that sometime in those past years, I developed an alcohol problem. I managed to stop drinking and haven't had a drink in almost thirty years now. Different people have different things that help them stay away from alcohol. One of the things I do is be open and freely talk about my problem. I don't preach. I just talk about those days and the stupid things I did and make people laugh.

One day at the academy, I was talking to some friends and I mentioned that I was a drunk. As we were setting up the props for the day's training, I was walking next to a guy that was newer. I really didn't know him well. I was talking, about what I don't remember, probably about how to set something up. I looked up and the guy was looking at me and said to me, "You're *no* drunk."

I was kind of shocked. I didn't even know that he'd heard me earlier, but I might have told him that I was one. But, it was good to hear. That same guy, later that same day, told me, "I'd follow you down the barrel of a gun."

It might sound corny, but looking at him as he looked at me, I knew that he wasn't kidding. This man was a decorated combat veteran and didn't hand out compliments easily. I remember looking at him, dumfounded, thinking, *"Who the hell is he talking to?*" There was no one else around, but he couldn't mean me. But he did.

That was the end of the conversation and nothing else was said, but that was a strong personal endorsement and it came at a time I needed it most.

Old Station 1

When I was appointed to the fire department, I was assigned to station 1, headquarters. It was in a building built in the 50s to house a two-man police department, a two-man fire department, and the town hall. As the town grew through the years, so did the police and fire departments, and the town hall needed more space. The town hall moved into a large unused school building and the police and fire departments shared the old building. It still wasn't really big enough, but new buildings weren't on the horizon yet.

Station 1 housed two engines, a ladder truck, and an ambulance, plus the duty officer's car. Every time new apparatus was bought, it seemed to be bigger than the one it replaced. Space in the building was at a premium–not as bad as some other fire departments I've seen, but crowded, none the less. We were on a single floor, so there were no stairs or pole. We had the bay doors open when the weather was nice and warm. There was a watch room where the dispatcher used to sit, back before a joint fire and police dispatch system was installed and manned by civilians.

Way back, we used to have screen doors on the bunkroom, the watch room, and the day room to keep the place cooler. We had an AC in the day room, but it didn't go on until it got really hot. I can remember lying in my bunk at night and listening to the train bells as a train moved slowly over the nearby tracks and the sound of sweat droplets as they fell from the four guys trying to sleep. After a while, we got through-the-window ACs for the watch room and bunkroom. Comfort is a subjective thing, so that created a whole new set of problems, but the sound of sweat droplets through the night disappeared.

I remember being the desk man, and in my early winters, the big overhead doors had a release on a hanging rope. One had to pull on the rope and the door opened. When the desk man answered a call, he had to find out what was happening and where, get the right apparatus on the road, and then go close the overhead doors.

First time I did that was the last time I didn't put on my shoes right away. I had socks on and they got soaked by the snow blowing through the open bay door when I went to close it.

We did get electric doors after a while, and the last guy to bed would close and lock up the doors for the night. The first guy up in the morning would make coffee and open those doors if the weather was good, then sit or stand around and drink the coffee.

In winter, the heat often would break down when it was coldest and we'd freeze in front of rented space heaters. They kept it above freezing, but every time we had to open a bay door, we lost heat.

New engines that were bought for the department were diesels instead of gasoline-powered. The fumes are a proven carcinogen. Since the apparatus were kept inside the building, the screen doors disappeared and all the inside doors remained closed.

There was a stream out back and for centuries the water would rise up in the spring. When that happened, our basement would flood. We'd have to squeegee the water out of the police pistol range.

There was a cat that came to live in the building. His name was Gordon. He would come in through the firehouse and sit by the door connecting to the police station and wait for someone to let him through. I guess he'd been a stray and someone started feeding him. He was with us for years until he was very old. I think he might have died before the old building was demolished.

Shortly after the floors finally started to crumble, a new building was designed and built. Construction lasted well over a year. Meanwhile, we lived in trailers and the apparatus were kept in a big tent. As luck would have it, I was the shift commander on the very first shift when the new building was used. It was a night shift and we didn't even have the place furnished yet. That night I slept on a mattress on the floor next to my portable radio because the communication system in the new building hadn't been completed yet. That was a seat-of-the-pants move from our temporary housing into the newly built building. It was too soon, but the powers that be insisted.

I didn't like that new building at all, now or then. I never felt good when I was in there. It was always too hot or too cold. Plus, the place was too big. I could go all day and not see one of the other firefighters. The whole building had an unhealthy atmosphere to it.

The doors are closed now; we can't have people coming in when we are all upstairs and out of sight. You know, that old building might have been a falling down dump, but it was a friendly place, and for so many years, it was home. I do miss it.

Fund Raising

When I first was appointed as a call firefighter, I was invited to join the Firefighters Association. It was set up for the welfare of all our firefighters, unlike the union which includes only full-time career people. The union had their ways of raising money, and so did the association.

I remember going to the firemen's ball every year. It was put on by the association. It was a formal event that was well attended and raised a lot of money for the good of the firefighters. There were some small things done to raise funds, but the ball was the big event. We depended on that to make money.

Then I guess fewer people were interested in a formal dance after a while. A few people had the idea to change things so it would be moved out of town and include a dinner. Memories fade a bit and I don't remember the little details. The fact is that I thought it was a stupid idea and I never went to one. Well, I guess that plan didn't last too long before the dinner thing was scrapped.

What would we need so much money for, you might ask? The association existed to benefit all the firefighters, both full-time and call. It helped when guys needed money in an emergency. They also sent flowers to members and their families for sickness, births, marriages, and funerals. I can't begin to mention all the things they did for kids, from Halloween and Christmas parties, to bringing Santa around town in his sleigh on a fire engine. There were other things done, like dances and an attempt to revive the ball, but they lost popularity.

Then the association got involved with a fund raising company that set up flag football games between our firefighters/police and some retired pro football players from the New England Patriots, as well as a few retired Boston Bruins players. Since the company took care of all the advertising and everything else, they took the lion's share of the donations, but there was quite a bit made, so the association got a good amount, too. I even met some of the current Patriots players. They were not supposed to play in those games, but some did anyway.

I played in some games, including the one when I saw my first total eclipse. I was lined up and looked up and saw an ex-All-Pro guard lined up across from me. He was so big that he blotted out the sun. In the end, though, he only used one arm to brush me aside like a bug.

Those games were fun, but someone was bound to get hurt…and they did. We had a guy with about six months with the fire department and almost no sick leave accrued. He was a tall, slim kid. The smallest Patriot or Bruin was much bigger. One of those big football players pushed this kid so he fell as his knee came apart. It was the old ACL. What to do? Well, the kid was taken care of. We, as members of the department, gave the kid enough of our sick leave days to keep a paycheck coming for him while he healed.

After that, the games became slow pitch softball. It was much safer, but it's just not the same watching a former pro football player playing right field in a soft ball game.

After I retired, I heard that there was another football game and another guy was injured badly and was out for a long time. I don't know all the particulars of that injury, but I don't think there are any more sporting events coming up!

For a Day in the Sun

The town I worked for has a lot of bodies of water in it. We have a river, several large ponds and many smaller ones, plus a lake that spans several towns. On the lake is our town beach. There is also another part of the lake and surrounding area designated as a state park. It has boat rentals and ramps to launch boats and a nice wooded area for families to enjoy their day, cook on charcoal grills, and swim at the beach with its lifeguards. There have been some drownings there, but for all the people who use it, there have been very few problems. There will always be accidents happening.

What had us worried were the overflow crowds that line up for a chance to get into the state park in the summer. There is a capacity limit and it is enforced. There is a major interstate highway nearby and the exit ramp is not a mile from the park. In the warm weather, people take the highway from Boston out to our suburb to spend a day in the sun and in the water...and they begin to arrive early. I have seen, on a fourth of July weekend, the park full by 7:00 a.m. and the line stretching back for a mile, waiting. Sometimes whole families will wait for hours to get in. Some get in late in the day and some not at all. That's unusual, but it can happen. Waiting in a long line in the sun with impatient, whiney children will put a strain on patience. I've seen state police on horseback there to help with traffic control at the entrance.

People have tried to park elsewhere and walk into the park, so they had to put a limit on walk-ins, too. Some people will park at the mall up the street and sneak in through the woods, but if they get caught, they are asked to leave the park.

It's not uncommon for people to drive up the road to another part of the lake. Swimming isn't permitted in those other areas and there is no beach. Some years ago, a family went up the road to one of those other places. Shortly after they settled down on a blanket, they couldn't find their two year old. The small child was later found face down in about a foot of water.

Strange thing is that even though I grew up nearby, I have never been to the beach at that state park—except for an emergency call or a fast cut-through to the mall when I was a kid. My family used to use the boat launch for Dad's boats, but we never used the beach. Being a denizen of the lake area, I've swum all over in many other bodies of water. We didn't need the state park and we didn't have to travel and pay to swim. Thinking about it, I'm lucky not to have to join those folks in line.

Parade Rest

We had a chief for a long time that didn't really have any rhyme or reason to much of anything he did. He'd go shopping and come back with things like computers or tools, things that we didn't need or want. He came and went as he pleased, and that was OK with us because we didn't want him near us at an incident. He would march with the department in the Memorial Day parade, but would always have some place to go part way through and would drop out. But for all the strange things he did, there was one that just boggled my mind.

I don't remember which day it was—some obscure holiday—and my chief decided that there was going to be a parade. He called some area fire departments and invited them to participate, and some accepted. They showed up at the appointed place at the right time. Trouble was, the chief never told anyone else about his plan, and he himself didn't even show up. No one in our department knew what was going on when the fire apparatus from our neighboring towns, tired of waiting around, started traveling in a line all the way to the center of town. They finished the route and then went home.

That story is absolutely true, and though we were kind of surprised and laughed at it—and still do—no one was shocked that our boss could do something like that. That was bizarre!

A Nicer Shade of Green

I used any connections I could to get training for the fire department. Sure, I could have done the same inane, boring things that all training officers had done before me. I know firsthand how dull that can get after a short while. I tried to get interesting things. I brought in a water rescue course twice. The SCBA maze trailer was brought out from the academy for training on how to maneuver around an unfamiliar space in the dark. The academy also has a flashover simulator that I arranged to use. Those are just a few of the things I was able to bring in. There are many more.

I spoke to the powers that be at the flammable gas firefighting school and they set up a gas course one day just for our call people. Some of the full-timers came, too. I have worked as an instructor at the gas school for many years, and I agreed to help out with the class. While we were waiting to check in with the commander, I was talking to the guys about what to expect. I mentioned that they would recognize the incident commander because he looked like Shrek, although Shrek was a nicer shade of green. They all laughed–until the man walked up and introduced himself. Then there were heads turning, astonished faces toward me. The guys were telling me that I was right. The guy was a dead ringer for Shrek...but Shrek really was a nicer shade of green!

Your Life Depends on It

There are many things on a fire ground that will kill you, some might be types of fuels and some might be a result of the fire's behavior. The behavior of fire is something we can sometimes create...sort of. Live fire training is a very valuable training tool.

A few years ago, someone designed a prop for us to train for a particularly deadly phenomenon of fire behavior: a flashover. A flashover is when everything in a room heats to its ignition temperature all at once.

Way back, just after the last ice age when I came on the fire department, there were few home alarm systems or services. The smoke detector laws were new, so not everyone had them or the knowledge of how they worked or where they should be placed. We'd get a frantic phone call saying that the neighbor's house is on fire and they don't know where everybody is. We'd show up to find flames blowing out the windows. The fire would have been burning unnoticed for a while, and a flashover had already taken place.

Today we put our firefighters in state-of-the-art fire gear that covers the entire body, and with a state-of-the-art self contained breathing apparatus. We train and equip them to go inside and fight the fire, if possible, face to face. Then, with the coming of home security systems and hard wired smoke, heat, and CO detectors, as well as home fire alarms, we find ourselves showing up at a fire much earlier than the fire department used to. Now we go in and find high heat and black smoke, along with some smaller flames. It wouldn't have reached the flashover point yet. Often the fire hadn't even broken out yet, so now we might have a new grave danger to deal with: an impending flashover.

It doesn't take a large fire to cause a flashover either. You could have a small fire in a full wastebasket in a room full of furniture and other things that burn. The heat rises to the ceiling then starts to bank down. That's when maybe the drapes or a chair catches fire. The room fills with black smoke and everything else in the room heats up. At this point, the smoke is thick and black with little fire seen, but the heat is high. Then, when it's ready, the room and everything in it just bursts into flame. It is an awesome sight to see. The temperature reaches a thousand degrees nearly at once.

Anyone inside a room when a flashover happens probably will not survive. They say a desperate man can crawl about two and a half feet per second. Anyone more than five feet inside when the flashover happens is gone. But just being in the room, you'll be burned badly. It's better not to be there. Since we go inside to fight fires, it's important to train on what to look for so you know that a flashover is imminent.

The flashover simulator was invented by a Swedish company, if memory serves. I first saw one on some documentary and I wished that I could get into one to see what they were like. A year or two later, the state firefighting academy bought one. I was lucky enough to be one of the first dozen staff members to learn to use the thing so we could teach it to others.

First, we had to experience what the students would feel. Inside the simulator itself, it is unbelievably hot, but nothing like a real world flashover. The simulator is made up of two chambers. One is a burn chamber and the other is the gallery where the students crouch.

The burn chamber is lined with plywood on the walls and ceiling. A small fire is made with some sticks in a trash barrel. Just like I described, the burn chamber gets hot and the smoke banks down. Then when it gets hot enough for all the wood in the chamber to light up, a staff member will open a vent in the ceiling. It draws the fire, which blows overhead in the gallery.

I remember my first time in the simulator. As we were crawling out, someone touched my back and it left a handprint burn on my skin. That's how hot it got.

I continue to be impressed with that thing. I was able to bring it to town for training my department and it was a popular class, for sure. You might not have to worry about a flashover ever, but if it happens–like shit does–it would sure be good to remember that training.

Specialists

On my fire department there were three men who were called "specialists" and they received a higher rate of pay. One was the job of an inspector. The inspector was in charge of approving all building plans for the designated placement of smoke alarms.

The next specialist was the fire alarm superintendent. He was responsible for maintenance of the wires and fire alarm boxes all over town. When he was on duty, he would often spend the day out testing the fire alarm system or stringing new wire.

There was also a clerk. He did all of the chief's paperwork. He typed notices and helped type the budget, among many other things.

Another part of the clerk's job was to get the payroll ready for the chief to sign it. I remember a day when the chief was out and so was the deputy. The only one around to sign the payroll was a junior lieutenant...me.

That job went on for years until the clerk started speaking up to the chief about things that the chief didn't want anyone to know about, like how the budget was being spent. The chief wound up doing away with the clerk's position and hiring an older woman to do the secretarial work.

The last specialist was the department mechanic. When I came on full-time, I replaced one of the original four men that were appointed when the town first made a full-time fire department. That man, the mechanic, was said to be an accomplished pilot, even having built his own airplane. He was a good carpenter and a crackerjack mechanic. He was an old farmer type and was always puttering in the shop.

When he left, the man that replaced him as mechanic was another of the older guys. When that man retired, a guy who came on after me became mechanic. I'm not complaining. I'm sure no mechanic. This new guy was a good mechanic, too, but with a different mindset. He got things fixed, but there was a certain quality missing. Things always looked like they had only been fixed, never neatened or cleaned up. But he was good at keeping things running. When that guy got promoted to lieutenant, things changed.

I enjoyed going to work and I liked to keep busy, so I used to look around for things to do and sometimes that included fixing things. I would repair the recliners when they fell apart, and I would do minor things that had been left for the mechanic to do. It made no sense to write up a report for small things, like light bulbs, when it was easy to do it myself. I am not a mechanic, but little things, like tightening a bolt or a nut here and there, kept things in service and gave me something to do.

I once came to work for a night shift and was told that the ambulance had a hinge that was broken on the side door. Well, I went down to look at it and found that the problem was a nut that had vibrated off and the hinge had come apart. I found a nut that would fit and put it all back together, and the ambulance went back in service.

The next morning when I saw the deputy, I told him what I had done. He said that was good. But later, I was criticized severely for making that repair on the door hinge. There was nothing wrong with what I had done, except the mechanic didn't like it. Memos and notices came out demanding that all mechanical work be done by the mechanic. Hell, I thought I was helping out. There was always some work for the mechanic. I just took care of a few small things and I got yelled at! None of the other mechanics through the years minded, only this one. Sounds like it might be an ego problem.

Those Ch Ch Ch Changes

I came on the call fire department as one of eight new call men. There were already many older call men there who tried to show us the ropes. When I was appointed full-time, I was one of the second generation of firefighters hired since the beginning of the full-time fire department. There were three of us who were appointed then, and in effect, we were the first of the young guys that were academy trained. We took the jobs as youngsters, and short of high school jobs and the like, we were going to become firefighters. That was what we all wanted. The other full-timers had all done something else, and then had changed their careers to become firefighters.

When the department was all call–and even after–there were a lot of full-timers. Everyone was a lot closer. They all lived in town and knew each other. There was a togetherness that faded over the years as the department became more professional and those older guys left. There used to be a firemen's ball and cookouts in the summer. There were gatherings and Christmas parties. The Firefighters Association took care of all the functions and it was fun.

As for the guys, most were pretty good at the job, but there were more than a few that you didn't know what to expect from. There was one old call man who was a teacher and a call firefighter. He almost stuck a pick head axe into my head at a fire one night. He was on a ladder, and when he swung the axe back, he didn't look behind him, where I was. The pick head whizzed right in front of my face.

Back in the 60s, there were a lot of on-call people who got minimal training. There was a guy who was on his fifth day as a full-time firefighter. That night there was a fire, and long story short, several old call men left this guy alone on the second floor...where he was burned. He had to be rescued. I wonder if men who don't really know what they're doing can be blamed when something like that happens.

But as the years went on and the department became more professional, the sense of closeness, of family, disappeared. They are true professional, well-trained firefighters now. I often think back on the old days when the guys all were from town and many knew each other growing up. It's now part of a mental album of fading memories. I kind of miss those days.

My Last Officers' Meeting

One of my obligations as an officer was to attend the monthly officers' meeting. Under the chief that promoted me, the meetings were kind of informal affairs. A couple of months after I made captain, we got a chief that got a bit carried away with the formality. Each senor officer had to give a brief talk about a function for which he was responsible. I was the training officer and I would talk about upcoming programs and the like. The chief was adamant that all officers attend the monthly meeting.

One night, in the wee hours of the morning, we got a medical call for a child not breathing. We all got up and dressed quickly as always, slid the pole, and got the ambulance moving. I, as captain, followed in the car.

When we got to the house, the child was indeed breathing. The young boy was sick and very congested, but breathing. The thing I noticed was the dirty looks we were getting from the parents. They said nothing to us except what they had to so we could help him, but flames shot out of their eyes. I just let it go as parental concern. It was their son and when someone is waiting, a minute can seem like an hour. We were not slow and responded quickly as always.

After the call, we went back to bed. I got up about 6:00 to do my paperwork and reports before shift change at 8:00. I looked out the window and saw our nighttime dispatcher getting into a car full of other guys and leaving. I just walked into my office when I got a phone call from the fire department in the town next door. It was their duty captain asking about the call they sent us that night and how it had turned out. I got some of the story from him.

I found out that with the emergency 911 system, if the dispatcher doesn't answer the phone after several rings, it will automatically ring in the dispatch center of another close by fire department. So, the other town got the call and sent it back to us, but why didn't anyone answer when the original call came in?

Now I knew why the parents were angry. They thought it took a long time for us to get there...and they were right. All that transferring of calls took some time.

The next thing I wanted to know was what the hell was going on down in the dispatch center that no one answered the first call.

Lastly, I wanted to know why the dispatcher never gave me, or anybody else, any information about how they received that call. I called down to dispatch and was told that the next dispatcher had come in early so the nighttime dispatcher could leave a little early, but he left without telling anybody about what had happened. As the duty captain, I had a right and responsibility to know what went on.

To say I was angry doesn't do justice to how I felt. When the chief came in, I went into his office and shut the door and told him what I knew. He was really pissed off, too, and vowed to take care of the matter. He never discussed much about what he was going to do, but short of being asked other questions, I figured that was that.

We had an officers' meeting coming up two or three weeks later. It was only a few weeks away from my retirement. At that meeting, we all gave our reports, and when things turned to other concerns, I brought up that call. I hadn't heard anything more about it. The chief explained that the police had had an ongoing incident at that same time that required the dispatcher's full attention and tied up a phone line. In our town, between 11:00 p.m. and 7:00 a.m., there is often only one dispatcher who handles both police and fire calls. I understand that a guy can only do so much. He knew the phone call would go to the other town. The system worked like it was supposed to.

My next concern was why I was never informed about things and why a call from another town was the first I'd heard of what had gone on. I wanted to know why the dispatcher wasn't spoken to.

The chief came out of his chair and leaned forward toward me. Then he said, in a loud voice, "If you had been listening to me, you'd know that the dispatcher was busy with the police and couldn't have *known* about the medical call!"

I was kind of shocked by the chief's stance and attitude, but I didn't let it bother me.

That's when one of the lieutenants asked, "Then who answered the phone when the neighboring town sent it back to us?"

Dead silence. The chief just stopped talking about it.

The meeting ended soon after. I just smiled and thought to myself, *"Well, that was my last officers' meeting, no matter what the chief says."* What was he going to do if I didn't go to the next one–fire me? I was about to retire anyway! Treat me like that and yell at me in front of the other officers, will ya? Make me look foolish, eh? I said nothing.

That particular dispatcher was very good at his job, but had anger issues. He was a loud, in your face kind of guy. No one had the stones to confront him. I think the chiefs were afraid of him. But I complained, and because of that, that guy never spoke another word to me, except in the line of work.

Gravity Calls

In the old days, the fire alarm superintendent had to put spikes on his work boots and climb utility poles to do repairs and maintenance on the fire alarm system. Just after I came on the job full-time, the town purchased a used truck from the electric company for our fire department to use. It had an extension ladder that was operated hydraulically. That truck had lots of miles on it when we got it, and we added many more. By the time we got rid of it, it was leaking hydraulic fluid as fast as we could put it in. The whole thing was tired.

Then we got a new bucket truck. On the day it was delivered, we took it into the parking lot and practiced using the bucket. I had worked in buckets before, so I knew I had to work the controls lightly. After a while, it was only me out there when the chief pulled up and parked his car. I was finishing up and since he was watching, I asked if he wanted to try it out before I put it away.

He said, "Sure," and got into the bucket and up he went. That was fine, but when he started to come back down, his lack of expertise showed as he moved the control too fast–and came down like a fat kid on a see-saw. He got off of the truck, white, and with an odd expression on his face. He never tried that again.

Of Funeral Homes and Beyond

There is a street right off the street that I grew up on. There are no houses on it. It leads right into a big cemetery. I watched that cemetery get much larger over the years, and I started to know more of the names on the stones.

Driving in on that road, one might think that it was the driveway to the graveyard, but it is a real street with a name. It's on the old maps, and years ago there was a house on it. That part of town is old anyway, and so was the house. After a time, it became a nursing home. It was a hell hole and the fire chief closed it down in the mid 60s and it was torn down.

To the left going down that road, the back parking lot for a funeral home can be seen. It used to be the only one in town. It was owned by a company that had several funeral homes in other places. Looking at the edge of the parking, you can see a man-made cement pool. I guess it was supposed to be a fish pond. The pool is like an inverted cone and is deep enough for a grown man to drown in–and it seems that that's just what the original owner, the funeral director, managed to do. Somehow he fell into the pool one day many years ago, and due to the inverted cone shape, he wasn't able to get out.

That was the only funeral home in town for a long time until another one opened on the same street. The funeral director was a man who grew up in town, and all the old timers knew him. He could be a pain in the ass sometimes, and I've had words with him, but he was a funny man and generally we got along well. He had a way of looking at you that was kind of eerie, and his crossed eye gave him a scary look. He was pale as a sheet. His wife was a cadaverously thin woman who didn't say much and was also pale.

I guess he loved to joke around. Every Halloween was a treat when we stopped at the undertaker's house. He always had some scary treats for the kids, as well as a headless man seated at the door. There was a real coffin inside that opened and someone sat up and scared everyone. It was great, but there was more. Two doors down was the funeral parlor. He would make a really scary tour through the place. His whole family would help and it was great!

Each year, the Memorial Day parade would come down the street past the funeral home where the undertaker would stand and watch the parade. As it passed, he would run out to the street with a tape measure and take a measurement of one of our older guys. He did that all the time and it got raves.

The undertaker kept his place looking great, as one would expect. But I do remember a day in the spring in 1965 when they were converting the old vacant house into the funeral home. The back parking lot was nothing but big piles of dirt. My friend and I decided we were going to be archeologists. We set off for those dirt piles to excavate and find lost civilizations. Turns out, we didn't find any of those, but we did uncover a small animal skull and some bones. Not exactly Atlantis, but it was close enough for two young boys.

Where the Hell is That?

It was during a spring of heavy rain and floods that I found out that there is a dam in town. Now, I grew up there, and I worked in the town for more than thirty years, and never did I ever hear mention of a dam of any kind. That spring, things got bad enough region-wide that there were indeed dams that broke or overflowed. But a dam in *my* town? Never heard tell of it!

Then, a few months before I retired, another guy on the fire department brought it up and told me about it. It was an earthen dam, and it was about to overflow. I have no idea of what would have happened because it never did. It just faded back into obscurity. I never saw it and I still don't know where it is!

Among the bodies of water we have in town is a large pond. There is an old bar right on the pond that is reputed to be an old speakeasy. The area around the pond is built up now, and there are some valuable waterfront properties there. There used to be many little dirt roads leading to cottages for rent. Back in the 20s, my town was very much country and people from the city would rent the cottages and spend vacations there. Many of the old cottages still stand and people live there all year round. Due to the age of the cottages, many had septic waste draining right into the pond, but after some years, the powers that be took care of that problem and put an end to it.

They used to let ski boats on the pond, too. I had been water skiing there many times. The pond looks big, but with all the people boating on it, it became very dirty. I knew a family who had a dock and a power boat that their teenage son used to use. One day, I watched as the kid pulled the boat up to the dock. He went to cut back on the throttle, but he went the wrong way and drove the boat up onto the shore quite a ways. His father wasn't pleased and that was the last of that boat that I ever saw. Finally, the town stopped allowing power boats on the pond and now it is starting to recover.

Those little dirt roads I talked about all have names, and although the rental cottages went away, many of those little streets remained. We call them "paper streets." They exist only on paper: maps and the town atlas. Some of the paper streets even have a street sign on them with their name, but looking at them, you can tell that the road goes nowhere. There is one that I have seen lately that has a name, and really all it is, is a boat launching ramp next to someone's house.

The older guys on the fire department used to throw out the name of one of those paper streets to try to mess with the new guys. We even had an older man on the fire department who just didn't know where a certain street was. It was one of those paper streets and he lived right next to it! Part of what he thought was his dirt driveway was really the road. Over the years, the talk of paper streets diminished with the retirement of the older guys and the youngsters don't know the history behind the area.

There is now an association of property owners around that pond that keeps a close eye on what happens on it and tries to keep it clean and control the weeds. The fire department made a big splash with that association once a few years back. We had some kind of a program going on that required us to put a vegetable dye in the water carried in the fire engine to make it easier to see. After the program was over, a man drove the engine down to the pond and started to release the dyed water into the pond. It was all harmless, but they forgot to clear things with the denizens of the pond. They saw an odd-colored liquid being sprayed and they went out of their minds! What a scandal. It took some time to convince them that the dyed water was harmless. In the end, I guess they believed us, but we never did anything like that again!

Always a Target

Until pretty late in my career in the fire department, we sat on hand-me-down furniture in the station. Someone would get a new living room set and donate the old stuff to the fire department. From time to time, we would have more furniture than we needed. That was OK, though. None of it was new in the first place, and it cost us nothing. The stuff took a beating at the firehouse.

We were overstocked one day and had furniture along the wall and another row in front of that across the middle of the room. I was sitting in a chair against the wall reading when the captain walked in. He walked to one of the front row of chairs. There was a TV remote on the arm. The captain picked up the remote and chose a channel. Then he turned to the chair and sat, having taken his eye off of the TV for a second or two. That was enough time for me to pick up the other remote that was near me and change the channel. The captain looked up and cursed as he picked up his remote again and found his channel. He looked away to put the remote down, and I flipped the channels again. When he looked up, he really cursed and asked WTF? He found his show again and again he looked away for a second, giving me time to do it again. He had no idea what was wrong. He stood up and swore; he's not a very patient man.

He finally looked up and saw me stifling a laugh with tears pouring from my eyes. I was caught! The captain called me a foul name and found his channel again, but the jig was up. He was always a sucker for something like that!

Hearing the Voices

We once had a chief that was a slob. He just didn't put things away since he didn't have a place for anything. His desk was piled very high with papers and letters and mail and any other flotsam and jetsam he could accumulate. It was kind of pathetic, but that was him and it didn't affect me...until it did.

I was working one day when late in the afternoon I needed something from the chief. Just what I needed escapes me now, but it was important and the chief was nowhere to be found. He often got into his car and left for who-knows-where, but now I needed something. I went into his office; he never locked it. Funny story is connected to that, too. The chief always lost the key and would ask one of the guys to break into his office. It was an easy task for people skilled at breaking into places. Finally, though, he just left the office open–and often with the door wide open.

Well, I went in and started to look around. I was thinking about where I might find what I was looking for, when my eyes spotted an envelope addressed to him right on top of the pile of crap on his desk. Not a big thing, except for the red lipstick kisses on the envelope. That really caught my eye, and then I started to hear the "Voices."

They said something like, *"Go ahead. Take a look."*

I succumbed to pressure quickly and picked up the envelope. It was already slit open. Inside was a love note from some lady in another state. I could have gotten diabetes and tooth decay from reading the letter and the red kisses on the paper. The smell of perfume topped off the message.

"Well," I thought, *"it looks like I've stumbled onto something forbidden here."*

I folded the letter up and put it back in the envelope. I put the envelope back where I had found it. I looked around and found the thing I needed. I left the office and closed the door. I thought it was in everyone's best interest to keep this quiet, and I did. I never told that story to anyone, except my wife on the day I wrote this. I know I shouldn't have read it, but those voices...

Strange Happenings (Screams in the Night)

When a firefighter goes to work at a working fire, there are a great many things that affect him. All that work leaves him tired like you can't imagine. The heat can sap strength for quite a while. Then there's anything that happens when emotions kick in...and the smoke...ahhhh yes, the smoke! What it contains can kill him now or fifty years down the road. I could go on and on, but one of the strangest things that ever happened to me, happened when I was very new.

Way back then, we had an older version of the airpack that was heavy. The early ones had demand units which made it so you had to suck the air out. We also didn't carry enough airpacks for everyone, so as newbies, we had to prove we could "take it." The older guys would give us a bunch of crap if we used them.

Oh man, how the times do change. Today, the breathing equipment is lighter, positive pressure, and more user-friendly. They maintain an airflow for you and pressurize the inside of your mask. But the smoke still affects us, because no matter what studies or experts say, there are times when a firefighter just has to take the face piece off and stop breathing bottled air. The experts don't do the job, and studies, even those that try hard to be accurate, can't calculate how a firefighter will react to conditions. No one knows, other than another guy in bunkers doing the job.

I learned early that taking in a moderate bit of smoke can, an hour or two later, cause tired muscles to cramp up and contract...like the hand suddenly cramps and gets curled inwards. It can be surprising how strong the pull is, but it's nothing that can't be overcome easily...it just feels weird!

Well, not too far into our careers, I was working with a guy who came on the job with me. We had gone through school together and had been friends since first grade. Some of his relatives had also been on the job. He grew up in the fire service and knew the ins and outs...or so you would think. On this particular night, we had a house fire—not huge, but we worked hard. It happened earlier in the shift, so after things were all over, we got a chance to stretch out and rest.

After a while, I was sitting in the day room with two other guys having coffee when we heard a blood curdling yell from the bunkroom. We jumped up and ran to the bunkroom and found my friend seated on the edge of his bed in terror. His right arm from the elbow down had spasmed and contracted. I guess that shit never happened to him before. He wasn't very happy when I and the other two guys broke up laughing! We tend to laugh hard at those little things...besides, we knew the joke!

Exam Time

When I first came on the fire department, there were twenty firefighters and four captains, plus the chief. Then the position of deputy chief was created. The deputy commanded a shift like a captain, but was the second in command of the whole department.

When I was a call firefighter, we had a line of duty death losing a captain to a massive stroke on duty. There was no exam for promoting someone to that captain's job. The boss just appointed a guy. There was also no exam for deputy. There must have been some thought on the subject because the next time a captain's job opened, an exam was given. I didn't have enough time on the job to take that test. I'd have to wait for the next one, and they didn't come very often.

Well, time went on and another test was coming up. Trouble was that there wasn't much money in the budget to buy a prepared exam and have it proctored. That whole "buying a test" thing is a mystery to me, but the chief bought some bargain basement exam and gave us a list of reading material. There was a lot of reading and little time. We only had about three or four months to study.

What the chief had bought, we found out later, was a NYC deputy chief's exam. Very little of what was in those books applied to us in the suburbs and we did not have enough time to read everything. People in NYC who take those exams will study for a year before taking the test.

When our grades came back, almost everyone had failed. There was only one who passed. He was a real book worm; not worth much at a fire, but he could study. Trouble was that he didn't have enough time on the job to take the test. The chief had let him take it for practice. Since that guy was the only one who passed, the chief naturally promoted the senior man who failed the test! There was no money to do it all again and so we had a captain that couldn't pass the captain's exam.

Then the position of fire lieutenant was created, and there was a test for that position. There was also another captain slot to fill. We had a new chief by this time. The new boss was unorganized and haphazard with the tests. He would have preferred to appoint a guy to a position by personal convenience, which wasn't the right way to do things. So he used some connections and got a friend to write the exam for cheap, and proctor it, too. The test was a joke, but promotions were made based on the results.

The people who passed the exams, but didn't get promoted right away, were put on a list for future promotions. The lists were good for two years, and then another exam would be given and a new list created. The boss continued to use the same type of exam each time the list ran out. I usually did well on the tests and often came in number one, but there were no open jobs.

After the next lieutenant's test, I ranked number two on the list. That list almost expired; it had about a month left. Another exam was scheduled, but a lieutenant's job opened and rather than wait a month, the chief appointed as acting lieutenant the guy who scored number one. The boss thought he was within his rights to make an acting lieutenant, in spite of the new exam scheduled less than a month away. It's possible that nothing would have been said if the guy he promoted wasn't an asshole and despised by all.

As soon as I heard that that guy was acting lieutenant, I put away my books and stopped studying. It's common for a chief to put the guy he wants for his next officer in an acting position first to give them some experience. Then, since the guy would already have some experience in the job, he would get the position. I thought this was just wrong, but what could I say?

I talked and let everyone know that I wasn't going to be taking the exam. I had guys calling me up at home trying to convince me to take the test. The chief called me one day when I was at station 2 working. He asked why I wasn't going to be taking it. I said that he'd already made his decision about who was going to get the job and I wasn't going to be part of the formalities. That's the way we left it.

Meantime, the union filed a grievance about the acting lieutenant promotion. It seems that the contract didn't give the chief the authority to make acting lieutenants—acting captains, yes, but not lieutenants. The chief, who was always secretive about what he was doing and how he did it, asked how he could make the grievance go away. He didn't want to have to justify himself. He was told he had to demote the acting lieutenant. He just about ripped the white shirt off the guy's back.

Next time I saw that guy, he wasn't a lieutenant anymore. Then I heard what happened and I got out my books again and crammed for about three weeks. I passed the test as number one on the list. The other guy cried and whined about the test questions and how unfair the test was.

When I was promoted to lieutenant, my first day I walked into the firehouse and that other guy walked out. I walked out and he walked in. He couldn't get out of there fast enough at shift change. And things stayed that way for some time, until he was promoted to lieutenant, too!

The captain's test was another joke. The test date was announced and the reading list posted. There were three of us lieutenants that would be taking the test. The fourth wasn't eligible because he didn't have enough time as a lieutenant. I hit the books hard and did almost all of my reading on duty at the firehouse. It was the usual dust bowl of information, but I read it all. A big part of the reading was done after I went to bed if there were no calls. In my room, I'd leave the bed lamp on and lay on the bed and read, sometimes into the early morning.

The day the test came, I rode my bicycle to the testing site in the next town over. There were actually three towns taking the same exam that day and splitting the cost, but it really wasn't the same exam. The guys from the other two towns had two more components to their exams. My chief, ever the corner-cutter, didn't have us take the other parts.

I finished first of anybody in the room and I turned in my paper and left. As I was heading out, I heard the door to the testing room open and close again. It was another guy from my department, the same guy who had been promoted to acting lieutenant before.

He'd finished, too, and the first words he spoke to me were, "I think that was a very fair exam."

I agreed and went home.

After a couple of weeks of no news, I went to see the chief to ask when the test results would come in. The chief made a call while I was there in his office, and when he hung up, he told me that I was the only one who passed.

Another two weeks or so went by without any posted results and I saw the chief again. This time there were problems. Mr. Very Fair Exam failed and was blaming the test and contesting at least one of the books. He told the chief that he'd been to a lawyer for advice.

Well, the chief went to the union and the union came to me and told me that the complainer wanted the exam thrown out. He wanted something to be worked out for the promotion list. I told the union that I studied hard for that test. I read the books—no matter how bad—and I proved, with a good score, that the test was passable. I said that if that exam was thrown out, we'd all appear in civil court when I filed my suit. That's not something that the chief liked to hear.

The chief quickly came up with the proposal that I get the next captain job and the other two guys, even though they didn't pass the exam, would be put on the list in the order that they scored. This was unbelievable!

A captain job opened up soon after, which I got. My second in command was the lieutenant who cried so hard about the exam. Ha! Now he had to listen to me! That was a double edged sword, though. He had to listen to me, but he brought an air of tension to each tour that he worked. I don't miss him.

Entrance exams for being hired on the job were interesting, too. I've taken entrance exams several times. There would be a general knowledge written test and a strength and agility test that followed the guidelines for civil service jobs. Those were fun and I always did well.

On my last exam, the list I got hired from, I scored third. The first two guys had jobs right away and I had one when a job opened up in about six months.

When we got a new chief, things got interesting. This chief must have thought he could generate money with exams. In the past, applicants from our own call department were given extra consideration because we trained and knew them. It would be the same now, except that the exam was advertised like never before, and a whole bunch of outside people paid twenty dollars each to take that test. A long list was established. There were names that I never heard before, and a good many that I knew. There were a bunch of our call men and they were spread out on the list. With all these people to choose from, when a job opened up, the chief naturally hired a guy from our own call department. The thing is that he never told anybody on the list who wasn't one of our call men that there had been an opening.

The last man hired off of that list is memorable. It was a long list and even being a call man, he couldn't place better than eighth on a list. When the test results would come back, he used go out back and throw his gear around and scream and be pissed off. Then he'd try again the next time.

People were hired and this guy was now third on the list. He got his job at last. The list had expired, but the chief used it anyway. He skipped over the first two people on it—people who had paid twenty dollars each to take the exam—and hired this third guy because it was convenient for him. The first two guys were not even notified that a job had even opened up. No one said anything and so the testing procedure continued as it was...until the next chief in the door looked for something more than his own convenience when hiring and promoting. What a ride!

The Right Tools Make the Job Easier

The Jaws of Life Rescue Tool came out about the time I was coming into the fire service. During my years as a call man and for most of my first year on the job, we had what were called Port-A-Power tools. It was a set of hooks and chains that could be used with a handheld hydraulic tool to bend steel, as you might have to do with a car wreck. It might have been the best available before they made the Jaws, but it wasn't great. I don't even know if any of the towns around us had a Jaws set, but even if they did, we'd have had to special call for it and that would have taken time.

One of the fraternal organizations in town decided to raise funds to buy the Jaws of Life with all its fixin's. They donated it to the fire department in a small ceremony and had a photographer from the local paper there. They told me to sit in the cab of the engine for the picture. I still have that picture in a scrap book.

We wanted to show the townspeople what we had. Twice in those early years, we held demonstrations at the town ballpark under the bright lights. We went through all the parts of the Jaws of Life and showed our expertise in using them. The townspeople were impressed.

We thought those early versions were something amazing, but as things evolved, those tools became just awesome. They were newer and smaller with lighter power packs for the hydraulics. They had a new system of having separate tools for cutting or pushing or pulling and such, instead of just attachments to the same one tool.

The Jaws of Life was manufactured by the company that invented it. Now there are many such tools available at a variety of prices. Each one is called a "Jaws," much like the way every circular saw is called a "Skill saw" by someone.

We used to get cars at the local junk yard to train on and cut up with our "toys." I've cut many a vehicle up in training and on the job. Now I think back and realize that I was there at the beginning.

Drivers

It has always boggled my mind since commercial driver's licenses became mandatory for professional truckers that the state or towns haven't at least tried to require the same thing for firefighters. Others may disagree, but when you take a guy who drives a semi for a living, he should be pretty well acquainted with the truck and how to drive it. The government says he needs to have a special license to drive trucks on their streets.

Then they take a guy who is a firefighter, put him in the seat of a truck carrying tons of water, ladders, and assorted other tools, plus the people on it, and tell him he can drive faster than the speed limit and in bad weather, and don't require him to get a special license. I had a commercial driver's license before I started with the fire department. I kept it until I retired. But I never figured out why, if for no other reason than the money that could be raised, the government never required that license.

I worked in the private ambulance business for years as a per diem employee. Life had me working a lot, but never full-time. I met a great many people there and most did alright with the driving. There were some who shouldn't have had a license at all, but that's another matter.

Finally, after years, my patience was getting thin with that business and it wasn't going to take much to get me to leave. I didn't have to wait long. The ambulance company had been hiring a lot of new people, so they decided to evaluate everyone's driving. I'd been driving ambulances, fire engines, and ladder trucks for years, and so I was comfortable with the evaluation. I was told that we all had to schedule a time to be evaluated. Half a dozen people at a time would take turns driving around and the evaluator would observe each one.

Then I found out who would be evaluating: it was an older guy that I worked with on the ambulances sometimes. He was a pretty good guy. He was also an instructor of CPR and I taught with him sometimes. What he was not, however, was a good driver. I used to close my eyes sometimes when I was riding with him. He was everywhere on the road and hitting the brakes. Ohhh, it was awful! He was also kind of the go-to person for management to use to do things like this.

The whole situation told me that: number one, they weren't taking it seriously; and number two, when they tell me I have to have *that* man evaluate my driving, it was time to go. I put off making my appointment until they told me I had to get it done. Then I went to the supervisor and gave my notice. I'm not proud and I know I'm not the greatest, and if they had gotten someone who really knew how to drive to evaluate, I might have stayed. But not this crap. I liked the guy very much, but all men are not created equal and that guy was in no position to evaluate *my* driving!

Vermin

I have heard from friends and neighbors about the 50s and the construction of the interstate highway system. When it came through our area, it crossed the many wetlands we have here, and in doing so, disrupted wildlife, and in particular, rats. I'm told that there were rats everywhere, and people even had them in their houses.

I have two memories from then that say that those stories are most likely true. I have a vivid memory, as a very little kid, of my father chasing a rat up the hill. Dad had a piece of 2x4. He got close enough to hit the rat and kill it. I just remember my father holding it up by the tail and taking it away.

It was in this same time period that a piece of monumental stupidity could have ended tragically. I'm about two years older than my sister and she was probably about two at the time. We got up early on a Saturday morning and it was still a little dark. I don't know what we were going to do. We were not allowed to watch cartoons when Father was home and he was upstairs sleeping in. Mom hadn't woken up yet.

We were alone as we walked into the kitchen and saw something on the floor. It was metal and I thought that I had seen it down in the cellar, hanging up. But why was it here? I didn't touch it, but my sister put her hand down on it–hard.

It was a small steel-jaw trap that father had put there to catch rats. Well, there were no rats, but it closed down on my sister's hand and she screamed. Father and Mom came down and released the trap and there was no damage done really. Father never took her to the hospital to have her checked out. That wasn't the kind of thing he would do.

It really doesn't shock me that he set that trap in the house. I don't think it bothered him too much that my sister got her hand caught in it, although he never left the trap there again.

Thinking back after all these years, all I can say is that it was stupidity like this that was job security for me as a firefighter. It fed my family for many years.

It's a Small Town Thing

The town that I worked in was one of a big cluster of small towns. The area has grown up a lot over the years and many professional people have moved in, but there are those of us that have been around our whole lives, or most of it, anyway. We all know each other. As firefighters, we would see other firefighters from nearby towns on calls, at meetings, and maybe social occasions, and chew the fat and gossip for a while. Some of the things I heard over the years wouldn't be said today when everybody is scared of offending someone.

I knew a guy who was a candidate for a full-time job in another town, and I knew two weeks before his interview that he wasn't going to be getting the job. I just found out in conversation with an old timer I knew from another fire department. I shouldn't have known that, and so I have never spoken of it–until now. The information turned out to be correct.

There was another man I knew who got a job in a close by town. The guy and I were not friends, but I knew him. He was older than me and I think he was kind of pressured by his wife to get a job on a fire department. I have no evidence of this, only observations. After many years, his marriage was in trouble and he was drinking a lot. I was told by people I knew that they could hear the couple screaming at each other often.

Around this time, I started to get asked questions about the guy by officers that I knew from his fire department. There was really nothing I could tell them, but that was OK. They told me things I wasn't supposed to know, like how it was suspected that he was intoxicated coming on shift and was actually drinking on duty. There were at least two captains watching him closely. They never caught him, though. It was widely thought that it was true about him drinking on duty.

In the end, his union took care of him. He developed some sort of cardiac problem. His union dragged him to the retirement board to apply for a cardiac disability. I have no complaints there. We take care of our own, when we can. Problem was, his retirement wasn't official yet when the guy died suddenly at home. I think it was another cardiac problem. Since he wasn't retired yet, according to the law, he was listed as a line of duty death. He was given a LODD firefighter's funeral with all the pomp. At least his family got benefits they wouldn't have gotten had he retired.

A Glow in the Darkness

Most of the guys on the fire department were older when I came on the job. There were three of us who came on together. The department had a couple of others who had been the "young guys" until we came on, but the rest were my parents' age, more or less. Newer guys came as the older guys retired.

There was a particularly unpleasant man on my group. We were all pleased when he retired. We thought we'd be running short staffed for a little while, but the chief had hired someone and didn't tell us. He put the new guy on my group and told him which night to start. We went to work as usual that night, and the kid came in and said he was told to start work. We didn't know anything about it, but here he was. Things could be straightened out in the morning.

Meantime, what to do with the probie for tonight? Everybody had some advice for him. I took him out to the apparatus floor and took him through what was in the compartments on the fire engine. The guy had come from our call department, but I wasn't the training officer yet, and their call drills didn't teach much. We walked around and talked.

I pointed to the jump seat in the engine and told him, "If we go out, you sit there. Don't do anything until I tell you to, and then do exactly what I say!"

I told him that if we got a call, to stick with me. At least the kid wouldn't get killed.

The first night was quiet and the new kid learned what we taught him. He was a kid like we never had before, with weird music and a lot of young person's ideas.

He was the first one that I knew of that couldn't drive a manual shift vehicle. We taught him and made him practice. His first winter, we had him doing starts with one of our manual shift engines. One day, we had him take an engine out to the parking lot. There were still chains on the tires; we should have removed them, but we didn't. We watched as the kid released the clutch–too fast–and actually spin the dual rear tires on pavement with the chains still on. Oops! The captain wasn't there at the time or he would have gone nuts. We parked the engine and took the chains off before it went out again.

The kid was entertaining to have to work with, but he did do what he was told. His problem was that there were no fires. Years back, there were fires enough for everyone, but fire prevention works and the number of fires dropped. In the smaller towns, one could wait for years before there is a fire. The kid wanted badly to go to his first fire.

He thought he had it one day when we got an alarm from a popular restaurant in town. We got there and we were told there had been a small fire in the basement. I walked to the engine and told the kid to "mask up," and I took an airpack for myself, too, and put it on. I led the kid downstairs through light smoke, only to find that there had been some sort of small trash fire, but a sprinkler head had opened and put it out. Problem solved for the restaurant, but the kid was going nuts. He wanted a fire badly.

Sometime later, he got his wish. I was working at station 2 with the lieutenant. The kid was at station 1. There was some kind of meeting that night that brought the lieutenant and me across town to station 1. While the meeting was going on, we were listening to radio chatter on the scanner from another town nearby. They had a fire and were requesting one of our engines to come to the fire. The captain sent us in the engine and told the new kid to go with us. He was thrilled. The lieutenant drove, I was in the front seat, and the kid rode in the jump seat behind the cab. He didn't know where we were going, but I did.

When we got close, we could see the glow in the sky. I tapped on the glass of the cab to get the kid's attention and pointed at the sky. The kid just lit up. His eyes were open wide and he had a big awestruck smile on his face. There were several engines there from surrounding towns. Truth be told, the fire was what we call a "dump fire," just an empty building and not much to try to save. The building was already lost as soon as the first alarm came in. It had been a small factory that produced something once upon a time, but no longer. It was located in the middle of a thickly settled neighborhood. The big job was checking the neighboring houses to make sure there was no spread of fire. A dump fire, yes, but it was his first fire. I remember very well my first one. I'll bet I looked exactly like he did!

Geography Lesson

We had an older guy once who wasn't the sharpest nail in the keg, and as it turned out, wasn't a geographical whiz, either. A few guys were talking in the firehouse. It was just general conversation when someone mentioned the country of Austria.

The old guy piped up and said something about Austria being the place where kangaroos lived. The guys looked at each other, and one spoke up and told the guy that that was Australia and not Austria.

There was a short silence, and after the conversation resumed, that older guy spoke up again, "Well, isn't Austria part of Australia?"

Worth the Price of Admission

One of the chiefs I worked for was a captain on another department before we got him. He had been in the fire prevention division. It didn't take long for nearly all of us to decide that he was a paper pusher. It's not that he was lazy. Hell no! He was always off driving around going to meetings and such, which was just as well because things were usually a mess when he was around.

After years of living in the old public safety building, we were getting a new one! This was going to be part of this chief's legacy. It also frequently demonstrated his lack of knowledge of construction. The boss sure did like to talk, and he did talk the talk. It sounded like he got all of his knowledge from a book, rather than from real firefighting experience. He also walked the walk. Problem was, he usually tripped over something. We didn't like to have him around.

As the building progressed, we would walk around inside and look around. Our old firehouse was a one story building. This new one was two and a half stories with two of the legendary poles! Shortly after the poles were installed, there were several guys looking at it when the chief came along and was going to show us how it was done. None of us had ever slid a pole before, so we stood back as the chief threw himself at the pole.

The boss was a big man, made bigger by all the extra weight he carried. There was a *<crash!>* as he hit the pole and the whole building shook. The chief had both hands on the pole, but didn't wrap his legs around like he should have. He shot down, yes, like a ton of bricks. There was a loud *<thump!>* as he landed flat on his ass on the ground floor, still holding the pole...and the building shook again.

Some of the construction workers looked over to see if someone had been hurt. The boss got up, and with a stupid giggle, walked off. At least we knew what NOT to do!

Not on *My* Lawn!

I remember going out for that old tradition of shoveling out fire hydrants after big snowstorms. Some of the residents are pretty good about helping out and will shovel out the hydrants in front of their own homes. We complained about it then, but it wasn't a bad way to spend the quiet time.

One day, I was out with another guy in a part of town that I'd not been to for a while to do some shoveling. This was an area with nice, manicured lawns in the summer and very high-end homes. The hydrants here were often located in a spot a little back from the street. The people who lived there considered that area to be part of their lawns. They didn't like having a hydrant there, but didn't complain...except one resident.

We pulled up to the hydrant at that property and I got out with a shovel. I stuck it in the snow and all it did was bounce back at me. That didn't make sense. I stuck the shovel in several more times and finally uncovered a large juniper bush that had been planted right at the hydrant. It had grown all around, making the hydrant inaccessible and useless. We made a report about it so they'd remove the bush and didn't think any more about it.

A summer a couple of years later, we were sent around the town checking hydrants for damage. I wound up in that same part of town. We soon found that hydrant...now covered with an even bigger juniper. After a couple of years, nothing had been done or followed through on. Not really surprising I guess, but they did away with the closest water supply in case of fire. Hope they never need it!

Not on *My* Lawn, Either!

For a couple of years before the starting at the fire department, I worked for a DPW in a neighboring town. There were quite a few guys working there. We did a lot of jobs that other towns contracted out, including road reconstruction and hot topping. The superintendent always came to these jobs to direct things. He could be a pain to have around most of the time, but sometimes it was for the better.

He was an old man who clearly had spent a lifetime doing hard labor, and though he was on the quiet side, he had an authoritarian attitude and watched everything that was going on. He actually was born in that town way back when it was just a small town. Shortly after he was born, his family moved back to Italy and he was brought up there, only to find his way back as an adult. He went to work for the town and spent his whole working life there. He spoke much accented English and sometimes his sentences were broken, but he could usually be understood.

This was a very wealthy town and they treated their town workers pretty well pay-wise. The "old money" was in roughly the northern two thirds of the town and there were some stately mansions there. Those people were used to having money. They had always had it and acted like regular people. Sometimes they brought out cold water or lemonade for us on a hot day. By contrast, the southern third of the town seemed to be young, wealthy people with a superiority complex.

One hot summer day, I was with the crew building a sidewalk on a street we had paved earlier in the week in the southern part of town. The sidewalk was set back a ways and it snaked through the trees bringing us up to the edge of the front lawns of the homes. There wasn't room to get a truck full of hot top close to us, so we had a man running a loader bring it as close as he could. Another young guy and I would wheelbarrow it in the rest of the way and dump it on the new walk for a guy to spread and another to roll. It was hot and it was hard work, but as a young buck, I was in great shape and didn't mind hard work, but even us young bucks needed to rest sometimes.

If I remember right, during a coffee break we had sent a man to the coffee shop and we were standing on the new sidewalk as we drank. We were usually careful about not getting onto people's lawns in that end of town. The people sometimes weren't nice. I must have lost my head because I seemed to have stepped off the sidewalk and onto the edge of the grass.

I was still standing there when the resident walked up to me. He took me by surprise when he started to speak rather harshly to me. He really berated me for stepping onto his property and messing things up. To be fair, yes, hot topping is a messy, dirty job, and I looked the part. I looked around and didn't see that I messed up anything, but the guy didn't want to hear it.

He was still talking kind of loudly about us dregs soiling up his property when the super walked up and asked the guy what the problem was. The guy looked at the super with a sort of revulsion with the super looking like he did, like one of the workers, but clearly this man was in charge, so the man started to talk to him. He complained that we were messing up his property.

Then he asked the super, "Would you want them walking on *your* lawn?"

The super said, "Sure. Come on over anytime. I got a pool. Come on over!"

That, coupled with the broken English, was more than the resident could take. He was almost apoplectic by his expression and spun around and walked away. He didn't bother us anymore, but the job went quickly and soon we were done, leaving that man with his precious grass next to the sidewalk.

The Bronk

My wife grew up in New York City and her family still lives in Manhattan. She used to go to the city to visit often. After we had been together for a time, but before we were married, she took me to visit the big city with her.

The first time wasn't that dreaded "meeting the parents" trip. Her folks were away, and so we had the apartment to ourselves. I got a nice tour of southern Manhattan by someone who lived there and knew where things were and where to eat and how to get around. I had never been there before and I was awestruck.

I had three kids from a previous marriage. They didn't live with me, but I saw them often and took them on vacation trips. When each of them was about twelve, we took them, one at a time, to NYC with us for a few days. We showed them everything we had time for, and since we made those visits when her parents wouldn't be home, we had the place to ourselves again.

I remember the time we took my oldest there. It was in the 90s, so when you drove through the Bronx, there was a wide median and it was littered with trash and burnt out cars. They've cleaned the area up since, but it was a mess then.

As we drove, my daughter was looking around and spotted something moving among the cars and trash. As it moved, she could see that it was a homeless person. He was wearing a full length, fur coat. It was all buttoned up, in spite of the fact that it was July and the city was like a steam bath. But though the guy moved in a human-like way, you almost couldn't be sure. My daughter asked what part of the city we were in, and I said, "The Bronx." I then told her that maybe what she saw on the side of the road wasn't really a person. It was a "bronk."

Harsh Justice

In the firehouse, we have our own means of handling things if there is a problem with each other. We have pranks that are pulled often, and payback can be a bitch. There is a line that we all knew not to cross, and we all seemed to know when to pull back and take it easy, but there were those who strayed across it.

There was an older guy working there years back, and he was a guy that drove everyone crazy. He was a thin, wiry guy with glasses and a big mouth that he didn't know enough to keep closed. He was working in our old firehouse, a single story building with a four-bed bunkroom.

One night, as the crew was getting ready for bed, the skinny guy was running his mouth about something for a bit too long. The other guys went after him. They pushed him out of the bunkroom window in his underwear. They then shut and locked the window. It was what the little prick had coming, but the trouble is, it was winter and there was snow everywhere.

The guy tried to open the window to get back in, then he ran around to try the door. It was late and the firehouse was locked up for the evening. The guy scratched at the glass and whined and even threatened—not a great idea if you want people to help you out. Finally, just before he turned blue, he was let back in with his teeth chattering. He didn't say anything for the rest of the night. Ya just gotta learn to get along with people!

There was another man who had problems with good relations. This guy was a police sergeant and he used to work nights. He was a pretty good guy, but he sure did like to bust balls. He was good at taking harassment, too.

One winter night, we were locking up and the police who worked the 11:00 p.m. to 7:00 a.m. shift were coming to work at their station on the other side of our building. The sergeant was walking from the parking lot to the police station when he got into some kind of verbal exchange with a firefighter, all in fun, of course. When the sergeant started to pass in front of the big, bay doors of the fire station, one of the doors rose up about a foot and the nozzle from a two and half gallon water fire extinguisher was shoved under. Our guy fired the extinguisher right onto the cop, from eyebrows to ankles, and quickly shut the door.

We then made sure the inside door connecting the police station to the fire station was locked so he couldn't get us later when we were sleeping. I don't know just what retribution might have been exacted at a later date. I have to believe that the sergeant got back at him somehow. After all, it was a cold night!

No Brother of Mine

If there's one thing that I don't envy the police, it's the drunks they deal with. They have to go to the bars and deal with inebriated people out of control, as well as the drivers who can be difficult to handle. Even when there's nobody hurt, an irate drunk can make things difficult and disgusting, and sometimes dangerous. When on duty at the fire station, we often get called to visit the cell block to check out those in police custody who might be injured. I don't know what the drunks think of themselves when they get taken before a judge in the morning, but I do remember a guy with a lot to lose.

I was the duty captain one night when the police made a traffic stop and arrested a very drunk, young man. The guy was short and wiry with very short cropped hair and an athletic build. He was angry and belligerent and seemed to be wound up like a spring...the kind of guy you want to keep your eye on when you're talking with him to make sure you don't get punched in the face. He was also a firefighter from a large city not too far away. He wouldn't speak civilly to the police. He seemed to think that his "brothers" at the firehouse should have gone to bat for him and somehow gotten him off. Hell, if I had seen the guy driving in his condition, I would have called the police myself. There weren't any injuries to worry about, so he sat in his cell until morning.

Just before our shift change, the police escorted the man through the lobby to an awaiting cruiser for his trip to the court house. For some reason, I had to go to the lobby about that time and another guy went with me. We were there when the guy was taken through the lobby, still threatening and screaming about how he was being treated. He looked up and saw the two of us in uniform and started to scream at us about how we suck, we should have gotten him out, he was a union brother and we should help out a brother.

Well, I don't know if he was a probie or not, but he couldn't have had too much time on the job. I'll just bet he paid a price for his behavior when he talked to his boss. This dude has a lot to learn about the brotherhood. After the display that he showed me, he's no brother of mine.

Mom

Years ago on a Saturday about mid-morning, I was talking to a plasterer who had come to price a job at my house and preparing to attend a friend's wedding that afternoon. The phone rang. It was a frantic call from my sister screaming into the phone that she couldn't wake Mom. She was so loud and panicked that I could hardly understand her. After a second or two, I understood and told her to call 911 and I'd be on my way.

Turns out that she had already called for help and the fire department was en route. I told my wife and the plasterer what was happening and I left. Not knowing what I'd find when I got there, I was thinking the worst. Being a firefighter/EMT, I knew what would be happening when help arrived. Working a cardiac arrest is not a pretty scene. It gets messy, bloody, and smelly with no room or time for modesty. Having worked a great many of these, I knew how things would progress.

When I got to the house, the ambulance had left for the hospital with Mom, but there was an engine company still there picking up. I spoke with the lieutenant and he told me what they had found. I told him that I was a captain on the job and we spoke as one professional to another. He expressed his sympathy and I went inside to see my sister. Looking around, I saw all the signs of a determined battle to bring back an arrest victim. I saw all the debris and paper wrappers that covered masks, tubing, needles, and IV equipment. It was all very familiar to me...but this time it was *my* mother. I had to stay in rescue mode so I could help hold my sister together.

She and I got into my car and we drove to the hospital where we were directed to a private room—never a good sign, but it was what I expected. Very soon, my other sister arrived and the doctor came in to tell us that Mom had not survived. My sisters came apart. I'm not really an outwardly emotional person. Combining this with knowing what had been done and that my brother firefighters tried very hard to bring Mom back, I kept my composure.

They brought us into the room where Mom lay for a final goodbye. She still had the tube in her throat and the defibrillator pads were still in place. I guess it wasn't a pretty sight, but these things told me the story of a desperate attempt to save her life. I was at peace knowing that all that could be done, was done. After a short while, we got up to leave. The girls were crying. I just looked silently at Mom for the last time, stroked her hair, and left.

Rest in peace, Mom.

New Apparatus

When I first started at the state firefighting academy, they had two old engines: donations from a couple of local fire departments. There was also one that they had bought new, I think. That was the best one by far, and before it died, it was the best living advertisement for a fire engine I've ever seen. With next to no maintenance and constant use, it kept on going until it was killed. The state made some kind of deal where that engine was traded to some small island fire department. They had to ship it over on a barge. On the island, the engine was stored for a winter in an unheated barn and the water in the pump froze and cracked the pump. I sure hated to see that engine go.

I remember my first day of work at the academy. They told me to pick up an engine and take it to be used for training. That was fine. I could do that for sure, but it was an antique and it was hard to use for teaching. It was assumed that I could drive and operate it without any problem.

A while later, the academy actually bought two new engines. Those two pumps were beautiful. They had all the bells and whistles that were available. They were delivered in the summer when there were no recruit classes going on. The higher ups at the academy decided it would be a good idea to have us come in one morning to familiarize ourselves with the new equipment. We ran the pumps and then all of us piled into the cabs of both engines to go for a ride and a chance to drive them. We stopped now and then to change drivers. When we had all had a chance to drive and ask questions, we went home, ready to use those new pumps for the recruit class. Short of an oil change or a repair, there wasn't much maintenance done and the pumps slowly deteriorated. Little things wore out and weren't replaced. After a number of years, the engines died. I have never seen a fire engine as dead as these two were when they were finally taken out of service.

The next nice thing in the door was a new 110-foot aerial ladder. It was a nice one–and expensive. The academy gods decided to make sure that everyone got familiar with it. Trouble was that the guy they picked to educate us was an office geek.

He loved to walk around in a uniform, but the fact was that he wasn't at all respected by the guys who would be using that truck. He scheduled the familiarization class for a day when the weather turned out to be foul and travel was dangerous, but the class wasn't postponed. Instead, they made guys travel through the snow to come from all over the state for something that could have been easily done another time.

I went to the first class and we were out of there in a couple of hours. Then they tried to tell us that there were three parts to the class and we only had been to one. They said that there was a session on how to drive the truck, one on how to operate the aerial ladder, and one on how to operate the pump. This is all stuff that the staff already knew. The kid from the office just wanted to strut in his uniform a bit. The guys decided that they already knew all this and they wouldn't sign up for another class, and no one made them do it.

That's the way they always did things at the academy. There was a rule that everybody had to certify. Some people would do it, while others put it off long enough so it was forgotten about. Then there would be newer people who came and never had to certify. After a while, the whole thing became a joke. Except for the burn building and the gas school, they didn't require any certifications.

The Emerald Forest

At the home where I grew up, there was a place we called the "swamp" alongside my yard. When I was a very young lad, I would often stand at the edge of my yard and look into that deep, mysterious, green jungle that stood across the high grass and marshland, with its quicksand and mudflats. It spoke of hidden dangers for those who would dare attempt to cross the marsh.

The forest on the other side was green and beautiful, with dangers all its own. No doubt there were strange beasts to be battled, new things to be discovered, as well as untold riches to be had by the one who would take the risk and enter that beautiful and mysterious realm. Perhaps there were as yet undiscovered tribes of natives there. They might have never seen another human being outside of their emerald forest. Would they be friendly or hostile? I didn't know. I was filled with awe and fear as I would look across the marsh and imagine what might lie in wait for the unwary explorer.

After a number of years, I began to plan. I planned an adventure. I would lead an expedition into that dark, green forest. I would explore it. I would conquer it. I would be crowned the king of all people living there. We would discover all that was there and receive all the riches contained in that mysterious world. I found no one who had ever been in there, so I had no information to guide me.

One day, I got two friends and we gathered all that we thought necessary for our journey of exploration and conquest. I remember we brought a big blanket to sit on when we needed to rest. We brought crackers and water to sustain us for our journey. We had our guns to protect ourselves—toys yes, but to kids of our age, very real, or real enough to protect ourselves. We brought rubber hunting knives because, as we all knew, one needed a knife to safari into the unknown. Having gotten all our equipment together, we set out.

Crossing the marsh, we came upon a stream. We constructed a bridge of bundles of the high grass that grew all around us. Crossing the bridge and into the forest, I found it to be everything that I had hoped. It was dark, green, and beautiful. We explored for a whole day. We found no tribes or treasure, but what we did find was enough to excite our young minds. We had discovered what had been uncharted up to that time. We were the first to enter! Or so we thought.

Exploring and finding our way around, we soon knew every square inch of that beautiful place. We played there often and took shortcuts through there on paths that we had made. We brought friends there, and soon there were kids playing there very often, me among them.

Before too much time had passed, it was all gone. My beautiful green jungle disappeared. It was exploited and abused and vanished. The high grass was gone, trampled down by us walking through it. The stream was full of junk: sticks, twigs, grass, and yes, some litter. We had taken my beautiful, mysterious place and destroyed it. I often think of that place and what it was and I'm filled with regret at not having taken more care of what I had. We ruined it, and for what? I wish we had stayed out of there.

This story is true. Interesting that though vastly smaller in scale, there are many parallels between my story and what the European explorers did to much of the world that they "discovered" over several hundred years.

Driving Exploits

There were a couple of times that I won "Shithead of the Month" for my driving exploits. One day, I was backing an engine into headquarters. I was kind of new still, but I had a lot of time driving trucks. I kept watching the driver's mirror as I backed up in a straight line. I knew my partner had gotten out of the engine, but I didn't know he had left his door open. Why? Who the hell can say, but I stopped quickly at the sound of the first aid equipment locker being crushed, and its contents spread all over the apparatus floor. Well, I got my ass chewed and I deserved it; I knew better. Lesson learned, and you know, the captain fixed that locker and it stood until they tore the building down—testimony to not paying attention.

Another time, I was working at the academy. It was getting late in the day so I decided to back an engine into the firehouse for the night. There was no other vehicle in there. The lights were off, but I thought I could see alright. Backing in, I was suddenly startled at the noise when I ran over a recruit's airpack. What it was doing on the floor in the dark, I couldn't say, but I could see that the pack was probably dead. They must have given the recruit a real reaming for leaving his pack there.

Nothing was said directly to me, but there was a rule established that a back-up man was required when backing. Not a bad idea!

And So It Begins

I was in the fire service for a long time. I was a firefighter when I met my wife. All my children were raised in the knowledge and customs of the fire service. They developed "radio ears" from listening to the scanner, and could understand what was being said. They knew the difference between an engine and a truck[1], and understood the fire department jargon I used when I talked about work.

Riding in the car one day during a two week vacation on Cape Cod, there was me, my wife, our daughter, and our son (the youngest). He was probably about five. It was hot. Everyone was tired. Most of us were cranky and everyone was talking at once so you couldn't hear yourself think. Someone looked out the window and commented about the fire truck they saw. I was driving so I couldn't look right away. My son started to ask me if it was a fire truck, and he was asking repetitively and rapid fire. Rather than ask for some quiet, I looked out the window quickly and saw an engine on the road with us.

When my son asked again if it was a fire truck, I just loudly said, "Yes."

He then said, "So, it's a ladder."

The little smart ass! He got me!

---

[1] A fire truck is not the same as a fire engine. A fire truck, also called a "ladder truck" or just a "ladder," has an aerial ladder and carries ground ladders. A fire engine has a pump and carries hoses.

WTF

I remember a fine night years ago. I was sleeping soundly at the firehouse. It was a quiet night generally and I went to bed at 10:00, the time when the rules permitted us to hit the sack. I was one of three firefighter/EMTs working with one captain. The whole on-duty group was there, so if we had to go out on a call, there would be one man (my group had no women) left behind manning the firehouse. I was assigned to be on the ambulance that night. Very soon, I was sailing down Moon River, and having arrived in la-la land, was dead to the world. Most nights weren't quiet like that, but sometime after 0200, the tone went off, telling us we had a medical emergency to respond to with the ambulance.

I kicked the blanket off, swung out my legs, and put my feet on the floor. The other guys were starting to get dressed quickly. You'd be surprised and proud at how quickly a crew can get from a dead sleep to on the road responding. Well, anyway, I bent down to pick up my socks and...I couldn't. Both of my arms were asleep...numb as a dead fish, or anything else dead, I suppose. I guess I had somehow been sleeping on both arms. Both were unusable from elbow to finger tips.

My eyes opened wide and I yelled something like, "Holy shit!" I couldn't even grip a sock to put it on, let alone pants. It really would have been comical, but for the other guys watching. They were dressed and ready and I couldn't pick up my clothes. So, the other guys took the call. It was something minor, and I was glad of that.

Well, the ambulance hit the road, along with the car with the captain, and I frantically tried to get feeling back in my arms. Do you know how it's kind of minor agony as the blood flows and feeling returns? I got dressed as soon as I could, and when the ambulance returned, we got it back in service. Everyone got a big bang out of things when I explained myself, and I suffered some abuse at the hands of the rest of the crew. All part of the culture!

A Ghost from the Past

I am amazed and appalled at the number of firefighters I have personally known who have died from cancer. There were old ones and younger ones. Regardless of what type of cancer, it always seems to be a fast moving type. We do the best we can to keep ourselves safe, but firefighting is a dirty, dangerous job. Many people who don't understand the job or the culture tell us how we should do our jobs, not realizing that what they are saying is not possible.

Back in the very early 80s, I went to work per diem at a local ambulance company. Among the guys I met there was a laid-off firefighter from a large town a little ways from here. I'm not sure if he was married or not at that time. He was pissed off at his lay-off. I guess everyone who went through it got pissed, but it's the newer guys that go first.

The laid-off firefighter worked with me several times. I saw him often, until he left the ambulance company. His reason escapes me, but I know it wasn't a recall to duty. After that, I lost contact with him. I know he did get recalled later because I saw his name in the papers or heard it mentioned for one reason or another; the fire department is a close family. I also know he was the union president at one time.

In the late 80s, I worked with an older guy at my own firehouse whose son came into some money. The father kept telling me all about things as they happened. He wasn't happy about his son's plan to invest some of that money in a partnership in a health club. Dad was right…it did indeed fold up. He mentioned the name of his son's investment partner who was a firefighter in another town. He had the same name as the guy I used to know. After some questioning, I was able to find out that it was the same guy from the ambulance company. I found out later that the guy had been diagnosed with terminal job-related cancer. There wasn't really much news about him until he died.

Now, fast forward a few years. My daughter was in the tenth grade. Being the daughter of a firefighter, she often wore fire department t-shirts to school. One day, her math teacher inquired about a shirt she was wearing. It was an FDNY shirt;

our family has many. He asked if she had a relative on the job. She answered that her dad was a retired firefighter. He said that his dad had been a firefighter, too, and told her what town he had worked in. She came home and told us about it. I said that I didn't know anyone from that department...unless his name was...and I said the guy's name.

Turns out that the guy I once knew in the ambulance company was this teacher's dad. Since I knew his dad, we decided to e-mail the teacher. I told him that I had known his dad...perhaps not really well, but better than his son. The teacher told us that he was only five when his dad died and his brother was eight. He asked if I could write up a little story of how I knew him and what he was like, etc. I very gladly wrote a nice memory for him and his brother. I liked his dad very much, and it was my pleasure to help his son see what kind of a man he was...and he was a firefighter!

In recent years, we've done better keeping our people healthy. Not too many years ago, the average life span of a firefighter after retirement was five years. That has vastly improved, but cancer is still there, and each year when new chemicals are introduced to mankind, it gets worse. Rest in peace old friends, your tour is over.

> Dear Lew,
>
> Thank you so much for writing a note for my brother. See, my brother was only 8 when my dad passed, and I was only 5, so these are chances for us to "meet him."

Info Unlooked For

Everyone has an opinion and often people don't want to hear anyone else's opinion. It seems that every time I went to work, I met someone who thought they knew my job better than me. However, not all opinions and advice are crap. Sometimes a little tip and some good advice can take you a long way.

Many years ago, there was a Texaco gas station in my town. It's still there, but has been closed for years. Before that, it was another brand of gas, but from about my senior year in high school until a few years after graduation, it was a Texaco station. The place had changed hands many times, but at one point it was owned by a man named Jim. He was about seven feet tall–no shit–and he had brought a bunch of his friends to work at the station.

I also had a close friend working there. I started to visit my friend on nights when he was working and got to know the guys. They were a serious collection of wild men and we got along great. Went partying with them and all!

Well, there came a time when I wanted to get into the fire service, but I really didn't know how. I was trying on my own and didn't know what I could do to give myself a leg up. About this time, all I really did was to put in applications and hope.

One day Jim saw me outside the gas station and came out and called to me. He asked how I was making out and offered some advice. He asked me if I had looked into "this paramedic thing," as he called it.

I answered, "No."

At that time, I really didn't pay attention to things that weren't right under my nose. He went on to tell me that he's hearing a lot about emergency medicine and that looks like the wave of the future. We talked a while longer and I went home to start looking into schools for paramedics. EMS, as we know it now, was in its infancy. California had medics, as well as many other places far from us. In fact, there were no paramedics in Massachusetts at all and no schools offering the training. There was a thing, however, called Emergency Medical Technician (EMT). That was as close as I could come. I had no real trouble finding a course. Three of our local hospitals were offering the program. The hitch was that since this was a new thing, they wanted to train the professionals first, so you had to have an affiliation with an emergency service to take the class. Well, during this time period, I had gotten appointed as a call firefighter, so I was able to get into the class. I did well and it got me noticed.

There was a bit more time before I got appointed full-time, and in the end, it wasn't only the EMT certification that helped, but it sure didn't hurt. I think *that* advice from a guy I knew was what started things moving. Many thanks, Jim.

Spy Among Us

Across the street and a little to the left of the home where I grew up, is a pretty big open space that I have always heard called the "ballpark." I don't know how long it's been there, but it appears on some pretty old maps. There are two diamonds. They were baseball diamonds when I grew up there, and as I got older, slow pitch softball became the rage. There was a football field in the fall, and depending upon just where you are in history, an outdoor skating rink and basketball courts. The ballpark was a place to meet for pickup games of baseball or football. It was also a great place to hang around. A great many people played there and hung out there, especially as we got older and it was cool to just hang.

Generations of denizens of the ballpark came and went, and as the years went on, things took a downhill turn. There are always bad elements in every crowd, and the ballpark was no exception. There was always some problem with someone drinking or being loud or something. Sometimes, we at the firehouse got involved.

One day, we got an ambulance call to go there and found a nine year old boy unconscious and unresponsive. He had been hanging around with a group of older boys who were drinking. They thought it would be funny to get the kid drunk. They kept on giving him sips of some hard liquor and laughing until the youngster passed out. The older boys panicked when they could not wake him and we were called. That poor lad came very close to death from acute alcohol poisoning. That youngster would be on the high side of middle age now. I wonder if his headache is gone yet.

Things kind of came to a head when two brothers who lived across the street invited a motorcycle club to move into their place. The mother of the brothers retired and moved, leaving the house and property in the care of her boys. It was a nice place to hang out, too, until the bikers arrived. They weren't a biker club I'd ever heard of. They were every bit the outlaw gang. There was all kinds of trouble, from drugs to the Doberman pups that were found dead in a trash can in the ballpark.

They had been killed by some kind of injection to their necks. This all happened when I was older and on the fire department. The police had their eyes peeled for any problems—as often as not, creating more problems than they prevented.

One day at the firehouse, a police detective came in to see me. They had a plan and needed help. It seems that they wanted to plant a spy among the hangouts who could feed intel back to our little band of untouchables. What they wanted to do is use someone young looking, and to explain why no one had ever seen him before, say that he did not come from in town. We would say that he was my cousin from another state visiting me for a couple of weeks. He could also see everything going on as my house was just across the street from the ballpark. It might not have been the wisest decision I ever made, but I agreed.

It was kind of exciting. He'd come to the house and we fed him, though we didn't have to. He was a pretty good guy. He didn't stay with us, but managed to wander around and get the information he wanted. Then he left, and I never saw him again.

But the tales of the bikers and their antics continued for a bit longer before they were banished from town. I never knew the town could banish you. Sounds a bit Puritan to me, but the bikers left and things quieted down quite a bit, and my involvement in the world of espionage was no longer needed.

It Was All Good...Almost

The current firefighting academy sits on the site of the one that I attended. The old place consisted of several wooden buildings. It was one of those old depression era Civilian Conservation Corps camps that were part of the plan to get people back to work. It had little equipment and everything they had was all donated stuff. When we sent two men there for firefighter training, the guys had to stop by the firehouse each morning to pick up an engine that we lent for the class. Each student had to bring their own airpacks and extra air bottles. It was nothing like what the academy is now, but we got our basic training.

Sometime in the 80s, the three main buildings of that academy were burned down by an arson ring. Then the academy went on the road. Different parts of the training were done at half a dozen different locations. I came to work at the academy during that time. There was a lot of traveling to get to the different locations and the engines were still old donated pieces from surrounding towns. I worked support services, so I was driving and operating the engines and the other equipment. We had to drive those old engines to the training area.

Then the state bought us two matching engines–brand new with all the bells and whistles. The wheels of government turn slowly, but eventually the state came up with money for a new academy, too. The remains of the old one were demolished and taken away and a new academy was built on the same site.

I continued working in support services there for a few more years before becoming an instructor. I loved the work and worked a lot of hours. They liked me there. There were times when I was requested by the OD when something had to be done right. I had a good relationship with the bosses and the other instructors. I was there a long time and at least one guy used to say that I was a legend there. He wasn't really being complimentary, but that was OK. I *had* been there a long time.

As the years went by, many of the guys I worked with retired from their fire departments, but stayed with the academy to teach, including me. There was one man who I first met when he was a captain in a city department not too far away. I knew him when he was then promoted to deputy and then to operations chief. I always got along well with him. He was a chief officer and was kind of a pain in the ass, but I always thought that I could work for that guy. I always knew where I stood with him, and I was treated with a mutual respect.

This particular man was an assistant coordinator at the academy and seemed to be able to run things the way he wanted. No one ever said word one to him, no matter what new thing he instituted. He didn't give me any trouble; I did my job and kept quiet. I think he liked that. Good thing, too, because there was no recourse for the guys to address problems with him. Anybody with anything to say to or about the guy would put himself on borrowed time.

Still, I didn't have any problems...until the man retired from his department and spent a lot more time at the academy. The word had spread that he was kind of a prick on the job and the guys were scared of him. When he retired and left his fire department, he no longer had that outlet for his bullshit, so he brought it to the academy. He became a real pain in the butt as he watched the goings-on and commented. He pissed off a good many very good instructors.

One day, the class was ready for phase one burns. Phase one burns are very small fires that burn fast. If you didn't watch things and pace yourself, you could finish very early and earn the wrath of the recruit program administration.

I was in command all week for those burns and we did indeed finish early. But, being the diabolical bastard that I am, I had a plan: we'd do a demo fire to show the recruits how to enter a burning basement properly. We built a big fire in the basement and we showed them the proper technique. It was a great demo and we did it with the students each day, but the last. That day was Friday and it was an early release day; they got out a half hour early. The trucks were also supposed to be washed on Fridays. The assistant coordinator reminded me to make sure I got them washed.

As the day progressed and we finished up, the other instructors wanted to do our basement demo again. I looked at the time and then around the yard. We had two engines we were using. There were two other engines being used elsewhere in the yard, plus two ladder trucks. That was going to be a lot of washing.

Over the objections and pleas of the other instructors, I, as the incident commander at the burns, made the decision to skip the demo and wash trucks like I was ordered. We marched down to the firehouse and began washing. We soon had our two engines clean, but no other apparatus showed up to be washed. I knew I was in the shit.

The assistant coordinator came to me and started to call me lazy and he berated me for finishing early. I was going to explain to him about the other vehicles not coming to be washed, but he was ranting. I've had my butt handed to me before, but not like this; he was talking loudly in front of the students and the other instructors. That was way out of line. If you have something to say to me, take me into a private place, but you don't castrate an instructor in front of the students. I saw them looking with wide eyes.

Yes, as it turned out, I was wrong with my estimate for how much time we would need to clean the vehicles, but it was my decision and I made it. I can say that if I was treated that way at the firehouse, our next meeting would have been with the union rep and a lawyer in the chief's office. He had no call or right to talk to me like that, but I said nothing. I walked away and fumed. Certainly he was out of line. All of us instructors were officers in our departments. We have all dealt with people problems and know that you don't crucify a guy in front of people…in front of anyone.

Just after that, I had a previously scheduled medical procedure and was out for a while, but that incident still bothered me. I certainly deserved better than what I got.

When it was time to come back to work, I got my schedule and saw that I wasn't booked to work very much. I had a lot more time available. I also noticed that I wasn't scheduled to work any burns, like I usually did. I went in to talk with a different assistant coordinator, one who had been a deputy in a town right next to mine. I asked him if any more shifts were available and told him I was available for the burns, too. He told me to wait, and he walked out and was gone a little while.

When he came back, he told me that they had another job for me. He said that I was going to work the burns, but not in command. I was to evaluate and help the commanders with my experience. I nodded and left. At home for the next few days, that conversation bothered me. I would have been pretty pissed if I had someone following me around and I didn't want to do it to anyone else. I worked with senior captains and deputies who knew very well how to command an incident. They didn't need me telling them how to do their job.

I started thinking about things and remembered some other very senior people that they invented a meaningless job for to keep them around. It was sort of like "You can stay, but you have to work doing this 'special' job." I thought it was pathetic when I saw it happen to others. It wasn't going to happen to me.

I went to talk to the big boss who liked me. He told me a lot of reasons that I should stay. We talked for an hour or so. I mentioned a few other things that bothered me, mentioning the problem that I had had with that assistant coordinator. The boss said that he'd have to look into that. He told me to take the summer off and relax with the family and come back in the fall, refreshed and ready to work. It all sounded reasonable to me and I agreed, but I knew I had resigned. It just wasn't effective yet.

I took the summer off and called in the early fall and got on the schedule again. A few things had changed in my absence, but it was all familiar. It still didn't feel right. I worked two days and on the third, I was assigned to help teach a hose evolution. I used to run those evolutions myself, but I have no ego problems.

Another guy was doing the talking to the students and I was listening. Training had started for the day, and so no one was walking around the drill yard or going into or out of the building. Then my old pal, the one from the next town over from me that I had known and liked for years, came out of the building. He walked over to us and spoke quietly to the guy talking to the students. The guy had a surprised look and said something like, "No. No problems."

The guy was a friend and told me afterwards that the coordinator had asked him if he was having any trouble with me.

The coordinator had said that someone had come into the building and said that I was giving him some trouble. That didn't happen. I take pride in knowing what's going on around me. No one had gone and reported anything because no one had gone into the building.

But guess who was working? That's right...my buddy, the assistant coordinator. Further observation told me that that "old friend" from the next town over was every bit the backstabbing, conniving bastard his guys said he was. I guess I learned.

I haven't been back there and haven't seen the two guys involved for years. I really loved that place the way it used to be, but I always said that when it wasn't fun anymore, I would be leaving. I still shake my head and wonder if the assistant coordinator really did have something to do with messing with me. I never would have thought so, but the times, they were a-changing.

Sheets

A firehouse is just that: a house where firefighters live, work, eat, and sleep. I can't speak for part-time or vollies, but most full-time fire departments have a bunkroom where firefighters sleep. There is one notable exception in my own experience. It was a small department which should have been much bigger, given where it's located and what it had to respond to. I had the privilege of staying there for a night on two occasions when I was in the area. (They saved me hotel cost.) They had plenty of room because the firefighters were not allowed to sleep in the beds. The recliner was OK, but not the beds.

I remember getting up one of my mornings there to find the guy who had arranged my stay. He'd worked the night before, and between the ambulance calls on the interstate highway and the problems during the thunderstorm that had rolled in through the night, he'd been up most of the night. He was glassy eyed and tired, trying to catch a nap in a recliner. He told me that it was a department rule that they couldn't sleep in the bunkroom. Wow...glad that never happened where I worked. Those 10s and 14s would have been a nightmare!

In my department, we had a four-bed bunkroom where the duty shift could sleep from 10:00 p.m. to 7:00 a.m., if we didn't have any calls. When I started as a new guy, I was given two sets of sheets with pillow cases and instructions to use a set twice, that is two shifts or four nights, then change them, unless there was a good reason to change earlier. The sheets were issued by my shift officer. When dirty, they went into a plastic barrel and it was picked up by a laundry service, cleaned, and brought back once or twice a week, as I remember.

It should have worked out fine and would have, but for some muckraking individuals. They liked nothing better than to cause as much trouble for the chief as possible. It seems that the chief at the time was concerned that people were not following the rules and the laundry was costing the department a lot of money. This linen thing got ugly and attained the status of a major problem, far outstripping its real importance.

We also needed new pillows. We had been sleeping on pillows with stains on them of who-knows-what. Yes, we had covers, but they were as bad as the pillows. We got no new pillows until the guys started using spare ambulance pillows, which were plastic covered and tough to sleep on. Then we got some from the prison system. The guys nicknamed them "chock blocks." They were brand new, and to be fair, they really weren't as bad as chock blocks, but they might have made a decent speed bump.

The blankets were cleaned and returned also, and after a while had shrunk up so far that you needed two just to cover your body. We did get new ones, but they also started to shrink after a while. No new sheets were bought for some time and some of the troops questioned how clean they were getting, and so they brought in their own. They got creative, too. One guy brought in a set of Muppet sheets with Miss Piggy on the pillow case. I, myself, brought in a set of brightly colored flowered sheets.

Many brought in their own pillows. I happened to snag a feather pillow and kept it in my locker. When I left, many of the guys and girls were using their own pillows and sleeping bags. Maybe we should have done that years ago!

Banzai

My wife grew up in NYC. She went to college in my area and we met at a swimming pool we both used to work at. Even before we were married, I was going with her to the city to see the sights and meet family and friends. One lady I met was a friend of my wife. I was at her home and we had a chance to talk a little. It was probably more her friendship with my wife than my charming personality that got us invited to her wedding. The wedding was to take place in Wolfeboro, New Hampshire on Labor Day weekend. As a matter of perspective, all weddings are nice, I guess. But this one really outstripped all others that I have been a guest at. It was magnificent.

Wolfeboro is a summer town with many people owning cottages and houses on the big lake. Labor Day is a big get-away weekend always, but it is also the time many people choose to close up their cottages for the season. It was crowded and traffic was heavy. We called around and managed to book the only motel room around for miles. It sure wasn't a great place, but I think it would have kept the rain off if it had rained!

The bride's family owned two houses, side by side, right on the big lake. The night before the wedding, there was a gathering there. The bride's mother was a Pilipino national and the groom was a Japanese national. Between the two houses that night there was a feast of Pilipino and Japanese food served buffet style out by the lake. The night was fantastic.

When we were ready to leave, we couldn't see to find our car. I had forgotten how dark it can get under the thick cover of trees. You couldn't see your hand in front of your face. This was long before anybody had a key fob that would turn on the car's interior lights. I didn't see anything until I walked right into someone's parked car. I didn't know if it was ours and couldn't even read the license plate because it was so dark.

We went back into the house and managed to find a candle. We lit it and carried it with us out to look for the car. There were several cars parked along the long driveway. Whenever we found a car, we used the candlelight to read the license plate.

The candle wasn't great, but there was really no other way we could have found our ride!

We found the church in the morning. It was a small, quaint place with a bagpiper playing out front. The piper even played a song during the ceremony. When it was over, the piper piped everyone out and we went back to the lake to the place where they had set up the tents and tables for the reception. The food was, once again, fantastic with a lot of ethnic foods. They even had a rowboat set up on land and filled with ice and seafood.

Early on we found out that the caterer had forgotten to bring plates, but the bride's father saved the day. He owned a restaurant just a few miles away and was able to go and get plates from there.

Sometime during the festivities, I saw a face that I thought I knew. The guy wasn't close for me to talk to him, but I just watched him from a short distance trying to place him. Finally it hit me! It looked just like a guy who, in a movie I had seen, played a bit part as a drunk in a police station. But no....it couldn't be him. What were the chances? I started asking around, and not knowing the man's name, I had to find people who had seen the movie and remembered that guy. The bride and groom were busy, so I asked others until I found someone who knew. Turned out that it was indeed the guy I thought it was! I don't know why I remembered the man, but I did. I didn't have a chance to talk to him, though, before things were over for the night.

The following morning, the wedding guests were treated to a very nice brunch at the restaurant that the bride's family owned. Once again, we had a fantastic meal. We had a wonderful time that weekend and the weather was fabulous.

It wasn't too long before I met the bride and groom again, this time in NYC. Both of them are black belts in karate and karate instructors, too. My wife and I were visiting the city and we got invited to the grand opening of their dojo. It sounded like fun and it seemed to me like kind of an honor to be invited, so we walked uptown to get there.

The dojo was on the second floor, overlooking 5th Avenue. We were warmly greeted by our friend and then we walked around and mingled. There were many people wearing karate clothes, but there were also lots of people dressed up who were there for the gathering, and there I was, looking like a tramp. I hadn't brought any nice clothes on this trip to the city.

I looked across the dojo toward the mats and who do you think I saw? You guessed it: it was the guy from the wedding and from the movie. So, now I know that he didn't just stumble into the wedding by accident! He *knew* someone! But who? Remember that this is happening over the course of an hour or two.

Before I could say anything to him, I heard loud voices coming from around the middle of the dojo. It was a large circle of Japanese men in karate uniforms, each holding a small cup. They raised their cups up all together and screamed, "Banzai!" as they all drank. Then they filled the cups again and did it again. It happened a few times. Unnerved, I looked at my watch and wondered how much longer we would be staying. They looked formidable!

Years later, when in NYC for the memorial service of my wife's father, that bride came up to me to say, "Hello," and was surprised that I remembered her. She was flabbergasted that, when she asked if I remembered her husband, I said, "Sure," and called him by name and shook his hand. It was there that I told them about looking at those Samurai and feeling very small. They got a big kick out of the story. OK, maybe they weren't really Samurai, but I wasn't going to tell them that!

Hells o'Hammer!

Due to the type of schedule we work, firefighters often have time off during the day to work another job. I have worked many. One was painting houses with another man on the fire department. This man was a very nice man, well liked by all. Problem was, during the process that involves thoughts being transferred into words and exiting the mouth, there was some kind of problem, a misdirection in his head, and the result was that you never really knew what was going to come out of his mouth.

At the end of a painting job one day, during the cleanup, I asked him how they were doing. He answered, "Oh, they're working like the hells o'hammer." Well, OK.

This guy had grown up by a notorious chemical dump in a nearby town. The media had stories about how those chemicals caused damage to the people living nearby. He told us that we had to take that story with a "salt of grain," as he had played on the site as a kid and didn't think there was any problem there. Knowing him, I think that was enough said.

Once, when we broke for lunch, we were standing in a long line waiting to order. He was a couple of people in front of me, and when he got to the counter, he ordered a chicken salad on "cesarean." I'm pretty sure he meant "syrian," but that was enough. I lost it. It started with a loud laugh, and when I realized that I had a 4 inch booger hanging out of each nostril, I had to leave the line and go outside to regain my composure. I did rejoin the line, after making an ass of myself, but had trouble eating as I couldn't stop laughing.

One of my favorite memories of those days is the job we had painting the house of one of my classmates. We had to paint it in fire-engine red oil paint. We were standing on a lower roof getting ready to paint an upper wall. I was removing shutters and my partner was standing next to me, holding his paint bucket with the brush sitting in the paint. We could hear the telltale buzz of a large bee's nest in the wall behind the shutter.

My partner made a noise that made me turn and I saw a bee on his ear stinging him. Without hesitation, he reached down and grabbed the paintbrush out of the bucket and began to hit himself on the ear and the side of the head. Paint was flying everywhere, as I looked on in humored disbelief. When the "smoke" cleared, his ear was the size of a small dessert plate and there was red oil paint all over him, the roof, and the window. I was covered in paint splatter and ready to fall off the roof while laughing.

Cleanup was somewhat less than fun, but the sight had been priceless. It was always a laugh and a good time working with him!

Bull's Eye

I grew up in a dysfunctional family. Oh, it could have been worse and I had a better childhood than many, many do; we had food and clothing and a roof overhead. We didn't have too much, but we got by. Dad ruled the roost and wasn't gentle about it, either. I hated to see him home. He couldn't stand me doing nothing. He'd find something for me to do and made things worse with his yelling. Father didn't seem to care what he said during his rages. He was an abuser: emotionally, physically, and mentally.

One day, when I was about twelve or so, he was mowing the lawn. He used to mow for a while then signal for me to take over. He was in a bad mood that day, I remember. When he called for me, I figured I'd better not delay, so I went running over toward him as he mowed. As I got near, a rock shot out from under the mower. It probably wasn't as big as it seemed to me, but it sure felt big when it hit me.

Just where did I get hit, you ask? Well, right in the old bean bag. I went down like a marionette with the strings cut.

As I lay on the ground gasping for breath, he walked away from the mower and said to me, "I'm just as glad it hit you as anyone," and he went into the house.

Never asked how I was or anything. Nothing was ever said about it, but I never expected there would be.

Great Place to Train

We used to train when we were on duty. There were also programs available at the state fire academy. Places to train are plentiful, if you look. A county training school in another part of the state offered a very good technical rescue program. I didn't belong to any special rescue team, so I never took things like trench rescue or high angle rescue, but I did take courses in structural collapse and rapid intervention team (RIT) training, both more useful to me as a first responder. Structural collapse training taught us tunneling through debris and shoring up against a collapse and a bunch of other stuff, but RIT training was magnificent.

The powers that be brought in the heavy rescue company from a busy city a bit south of here to provide RIT training. Those guys knew their stuff. As you might know, RIT teams are deployed to rescue firefighters in trouble. For the whole weekend, we learned to rescue our brothers and sisters. We crawled through rooms and their contents where booby traps awaited to snare our airpacks and we had to extricate ourselves. We raised ladders and climbed them to take victims out of upper windows and carry them back down the ladders. We did searches and wall breaches to rescue downed firefighters. We did rope bailouts and head first bailouts onto ladders from the second floor.

All told, it was a fantastic weekend. I was beat when I got home and went right to bed. All in all, it was a great time: hard work, but a great time. It was the best training course I think I ever took.

There was another firefighter friend who went with me to a couple of the courses. He was a veteran firefighter, but RIT training was a bad weekend for him. He tried to do a ladder bailout and caught the toes of his boots on the window sill and tore both boots open. He tried to do rope bailouts. His gloves were soaked and he didn't change them, so as he swung out the third floor window and onto the rope in front of him, he slid down like a meteor. He got up, and lucky he didn't get hurt.

One weekend, I went to another course with two other firefighters that I worked with at the state fire academy. It was a man and a woman from different departments who knew each other well. The guy was quite a bit older than her. The two rode in his truck and left her car parked at the academy for the weekend. I drove myself and we met at the training area. Once again, it was a weekend of hard work, but it was a great time.

At the end of the class on Sunday, we said our goodbyes and I started for home. My two friends were riding in his pickup just a bit behind me. I passed the hotel where we had stayed and saw the pickup signal and turn into the hotel again. I thought to myself, *"Self, maybe they forgot something,"* and I just drove home.

The next day was a Monday and I was scheduled to work at the academy. I got there early only to find the lady's car parked in a corner of the lot where she had left it on Friday afternoon. Well, I guess they had been too "busy" to come get her car.

In the fire service there are no secrets for very long. I was soon asked about the car. They knew where I had gone for the weekend and who else went, too. The guy's wife wasn't too pleased when she learned about it. Things became scandalous and highly amusing for a few months before it all came to a crashing end. The two love birds split up, he went back to his wife, and she got married to someone else.

A Night Always Remembered

Back a few years, I took an interest in teaching EMS. CPR was a good place to start. I taught a great many classes, including recertification for members of the fire department, as well as a private ambulance company I worked for. I also kept a dozen or so CPR instructors certified and held CPR Instructor courses from time to time. Suffice it to say that with all this, plus the many times I have performed CPR for real, I know it pretty well.

One night shift, a Saturday–not late, but the evening was getting on—dispatch received a call for a baby not breathing. The dispatcher was an EMT herself and knew to get all the information she could. The one making the call was the baby's godmother and a registered nurse. She knew what she was doing and began CPR on the baby and told our dispatcher so.

While responding to the house, I was thinking about what we might need. I was the attendant so it was going to be my job to provide direct care to the baby. My partner that night was a man who I never cared to work with. He was not a team player and tried to do things the way he thought they should be done...no matter how stupid it was.

As we arrived, I told my partner that I was going in and I would "scoop and run." If I found a baby in cardiac arrest, I was going to pick the child up and do a round or two of CPR on my arm, the way it is done on a baby who is only four months old, and then we'd go. There was nothing to be gained by waiting for the ALS team to get there. Then I told him to get the back of the ambulance ready.

We pulled up in the ambulance and the captain arrived at the same time. I got out and ran to the house, expecting my partner to get the oxygen equipment ready and put a short board on the stretcher for CPR. I went in and the babysitter handed the baby to me. I squatted down to do a round or two of CPR, when I started feeling the baby being pulled on. I held on and turned to find the captain trying to pull the baby out of my arms and yelling at me to put it down on the floor and continue. That's what you would do with an adult, but not a baby. I turned to the captain and yelled at him to stop, at which time I stood up, holding the little one on my arm, and headed for the door with CPR in progress.

Then, who walked in but my partner with a long backboard (sized for an adult), a bag of long Velcro straps, and a demand oxygen unit that we didn't often use anymore and would never use on a baby, anyway. I gave him a look of disgust. I couldn't use any of that stuff. I headed out across the lawn to the ambulance and found nothing had been done. No lights were turned on. There was nothing ready at all. I got in with my patient and had to lay him on the stretcher and stop CPR while I got lights turned on, got the oxygen working, and put a short board on the mattress under him.

We started toward the hospital. An ALS team met us en route, locked up their vehicle, grabbed their tools, and rode with me in the ambulance, where a desperate battle was being waged to keep the little one alive. We wound up with a police escort up to the highway, and the police from the hospital's town provided an escort the rest of the way to the hospital.

In the emergency room, we handed off patient care to the ER staff that was ready and waiting for us. I came out of the room and a nurse asked me if I was alright. I looked at her and she said that she had seen that look before and told me to sit for a few minutes. Then the word came around that the parents had arrived. Not meaning to sound cold, but I just wasn't ready for a meeting, so we slipped away and returned to quarters.

I won't comment on anything else, but I know that that baby boy had the best care anyone could possibly give him. We worked our hearts out, but it wasn't to be. They buried the baby boy in a local cemetery and placed a stone with his name on it.

My family is buried there, not far away. When I go visiting, I always stop at the little boy's grave and reflect back on a night I wish I could forget. I've told my wife that story many times, and if she goes to the cemetery to visit, she stops at that little boy's grave and tidies things up a bit. I have sometimes brought flowers, because he didn't ever seem to get any. I found out later that his family had moved back to Canada shortly after he passed. They visited when they could, but that wasn't often.

Ahhhhh, the baggage we pick up. I recall that night like it was yesterday. I was disturbed by the captain's actions there, but nothing was ever said about it by either of us. That night was the first night out for the parents since the birth of the baby. The godmother, a registered nurse, was looking after the baby while the parents had a few hours away.

The captain had to stay and tell the parents what happened when they returned home. We were not going to leave the babysitter alone to deal with that. I never envied him that job. Sometimes rank has its downside.

Getting to the Bottom of Things

The town that I worked for is an old New England town where its history is very important to them. There are historic houses and roads and there are many stories of famous people and happenings. The local historical commission has a lot of control over what happens in the historic district. That district includes the center of town where there stands a large house that is privately owned. It is one of the old colonial houses on the main road coming through the town center.

One day, the people who owned and lived in the house decided that they wanted to have their home painted. They had chosen a shade of yellow. Since their house was historic–it even had a name–they had to talk to the historical commission for approval. The commission rejected their plan. They wanted to preserve the original look of the house and they stated that the original color was white, and if it was to be painted, white would be the color. I don't really know *how* they knew this, and as it turned out, neither did the owners of the house.

Well, the owners had someone take a sample of paint from the house, right down to the very first coat. Then they had it separated into layers and analyzed. I don't know where you go to have something like that done and I can't see it being cheap, but those people had the means and had it done.

Guess what? In the end, they found out that the original color was *yellow*! Ha! I guess those in the know don't know everything!

The Great Melee

You've heard of the riots of the 60s and 70s in places like Watts, Chicago, Detroit, and Boston? Well, we had our own little riot in the small town where I grew up. It wasn't about race or civil rights or poverty or any of the big issues of the day. I'm not sure it was about much of anything. It was just a fight between police and local young people who had had enough of what they saw as bullying and strong arm tactics by some local police officers.

In the early 70s, we had our own groups of yahoos and hang-arounds. They would hang out in front of the local pizza shop and around the ballpark. There were some bad dudes in that group, but mostly they were just young people who would drink and smoke dope and hang around and be relatively harmless. I don't mean to say they were completely innocent; there were times when they got too loud or rowdy. Sometimes local residents would be kind of intimidated, and of course, smoking dope was always frowned on.

Around that time, some of the old police officers started to retire from the department. We got in a bunch of go-getter young cops. Some were OK, but others seemed to want to make a name for themselves by running the local hangouts out of town. Some of them took every opportunity to harass and strong arm those hangouts, and often it created more trouble than it prevented.

One night, I was with two friends in my friend's car going to a variety store the next town over. On Main Street, two police cars from that town passed us heading toward our town, with lights and sirens and moving fast. When we came back to town, we couldn't believe what we saw. There was a large group of the locals in the street between the school and the pizza shop, and there were a lot of cops there from both towns, *and* they had their batons out and were fighting with the locals. It seemed to be just a kind of melee, just a lot of individual fights going on at first.

I lived down the street, so we drove there and left the car and walked back to see the sights. As more police arrived, they got out of their cars wearing those riot helmets, and I saw at least one shield being held by an officer. The locals were fighting back–hard–and there was judicious use of the batons.

One of our locals got a bright idea. He stepped out of the fight and went to his motorcycle and put on his own helmet. Then he waded back into the fray. I saw an officer hit him on the head with a baton six or seven times with no result. Guess that helmet did him some good!

There was a whole bunch of us standing around watching, when one of our more beloved locals started to walk in front of the crowd trying to incite the crowd to start throwing rocks. No one did that. They must have thought better.

I, myself, was just there to watch. I didn't even know, at the time, what had started things, and I sure didn't want any trouble. More cops showed up. Most were in civilian clothes, so I don't know where they might have been from and it still was kind of a free-for-all.

Then a state police cruiser pulled up and a very large state cop got out and started to talk loudly and give orders. It was clear that this man knew exactly what he was doing. From that moment on, the locals were losing. Some were arrested and put into police cars, while the cops began clearing the street.

When told to leave, I didn't argue. I began to walk away when I heard a girl yelling at a local police officer, a large one. In fact, this officer was, at the time, our youth officer. When the girl wouldn't stop yelling, he demonstrated his skill at handling youth by losing control and grabbing her by the neck and pinning her off the ground against the wall of a store. That's the last thing I remember seeing there. We turned tail and walked fast back down to my house where we sat on my front lawn.

Over the next few minutes, several more refugees from up there came by and sat to talk about what we had just seen. Shortly after, a police cruiser came slowly down the street and turned left in front of my house. There were probably eight or ten of us then, just sitting and talking. The cruiser drove right past us and turned left again up the next street. Three or four minutes later, a formation of police, kind of like one of those old Roman Legion squares, came marching down the street. They all had batons. They stopped in front of my house and asked us if we lived there.

We all answered, "Yes!"

They asked, "You *all* live here?"

Then I answered that I did. When asked what we were doing, I said that we were just sitting and talking. They told us that we had better do that in the backyard and stay off the street. It didn't seem the time to argue, so we dispersed. I and the two guys I had started out with went out back for a while to talk. Soon things were over.

The story spread over the next few days about what happened and how it started. It seems that one of the police officers, whose name will remain notorious with those who lived in town in those years, was strong-arming three of the locals. He arrested one, a very *bad* dude, and put him in the cruiser. While the cop talked to the other two, the one in the cruiser managed to get out, get his hands in front of him again, and attack the cop. The cop wound up with a broken shoulder, and the rest started when he got on his radio and called for help.

That is the story of the Great Riot, as I remember it!

It Could Always Be Worse

My oldest daughter is now in her 40s. I remember years back when we took an ill-fated trip to San Francisco to visit relatives. My daughter was only about 3½ then. She had always been a cheerful, little girl. She'd never been sick. Now this trip was ill-fated for a number of reasons, but the subject of this story is my daughter.

Very shortly after we arrived, she got sick. She started throwing up. She couldn't keep anything down and so didn't have any food or water for days. She finally got so dehydrated that we took her to the hospital. I was very upset, to say the least. I had taken my family all this way on vacation and a healthy little girl got sick and we didn't know why and now she was in the hospital.

She spent several days in Valley Children's Hospital in Fresno. They found no reason for the vomiting. They called it a "virus of unknown origin." She was absolutely miserable for a few days, with IV fluids going into her arm. We spent every day with her and I was always thinking how awful this was and feeling sorry for her and myself.

At one point, she had a roommate. It was another little girl roughly the same age. We were so concerned with my daughter that we didn't really notice the other girl, until one special day. It seemed to be the day that the other little girl was leaving. Her parents weren't there in the room with her at the time, but that girl saw how bad my daughter was feeling. While she waited for her parents, she walked over and handed my daughter a little stuffed animal–I think it was a squirrel–to play with. We tried to thank the girl, but found that she didn't speak any English.

Her parents came into the room and we went to them and explained what their daughter had done and thanked them. They told us their daughter only spoke German. Both parents spoke English well, but with a German accent. It turns out that they, too, had been on vacation in California. Their daughter had also gotten sick, but she was found to have developed diabetes. The parents had been out of the room because they were with the doctor, learning how to inject their daughter with her daily insulin.

Man, did I feel foolish, like a real dope. Here I was, feeling sorry for myself because my daughter was throwing up and dehydrated...things that will go away. Their daughter had something that will last the rest of her life, and yet they all found reason to smile and laugh. Their daughter was concerned for *my* daughter!

I guess the moral of the story is that no matter how bad you think things are for you, you can sit and feel sorry for yourself, it's your right to do that, but if you take the time to look around, I'll bet you won't have to look very far to find someone who is worse off than you. Maybe you haven't got it so bad after all.

Buried Treasure

Before I got on the fire department and for quite a few years thereafter, the furniture in the day room at the firehouse was something that someone else got rid of. Not that we went dumpster diving or anything like that, but when one of our guys got new stuff for home, the old stuff was often offered to the fire department. We also got some offers from citizens, too. Sometimes we took it, but more often we turned it down with many thanks.

After a while, we got some new furniture bought by the department in the form of new recliners for both stations. Well, most recliners aren't designed to take the abuse they get in the firehouse, and it wasn't too long before the chairs broke or screws came loose. I used to repair them and spent a lot of time doing it so we'd have usable chairs.

The first time I turned one of those chairs over to fix it, a handful of coins fell onto the floor...a lot of them! After that day, I would raid the chairs from time to time and always found several dollars in change. Sometimes I found other things, like pocket knives or wristwatches. People usually missed these and wanted them back, but the coins no one ever claimed. Whenever I checked for coins, I never came up empty-handed.

Another place I used to scavenge for goodies was in the junk cars we would have delivered for extrication training. Often, I was working when the junkyard dropped off the cars and I went right out to look through them. Those things were a treasure trove of coins that people dropped and never looked for and other things they left in the car when it was junked. I got many nice hand tools, jacks, drinking glasses, and a whole bunch of things. It's always nice to find money and goodies, but I have to admit, even the searching was fun.

A Gift of Love

One time, we had a deputy chief who got his chops busted continuously. Working in a smaller department, we had a more relaxed relationship with our officers, as long as it was joking and out of the eye of the public.

Well, this deputy was short and bald and applied a certain "down home" logic to things. I, with my big mouth, had something to say, as usual, when he came in all smiles one day. It was his birthday and his wife had bought him a ride in a glider. He was all tickled to schedule it.

Then I said to him, "Hey Dep., everything OK at home?"

He looked at me and asked what I meant.

I said something like, "For your birthday your wife gave you a ride in a plane with no motor? Think the honeymoon might be over?"

He walked away, shaking his head.

Why We Test

We test all of our hoses each year in the fall. It's a big job, but each shift does its part and it gets done. There have been a few mishaps, but it's usually just a long day. This, like many fire department duties, can be a little dangerous with the high pressure being used, but we gotta make sure the hose can take it when we need it for firefighting.

There was a time when it got me. At that time, I was working at station 2 with a man who was older than my father who I intensely disliked. We worked in a two-man house and so I usually just kept quiet and didn't say anything to him and let him rant...whatever. There was nothing I had to say to him, anyway.

We went to headquarters one day to test hose. We got all the hose off the engine and stretched it all out in hundred-foot lengths and hooked the engine up to a hydrant. To test the hoses, we put nozzles on two of them at a time and hook them up to the pump and slowly increase pressure to 250 psi, as I remember. We'd hold it there for a short time and check for leaks or breaks or damage. Then we reduce the pressure at the pump, bleed the hoses by opening the nozzles, then move on to the next two hoses.

This particular day I was running my pump. I was all hooked up and slowly increasing pressure, when a 2.5" line burst about six inches out from the pump. That's what we look for, but this time I couldn't get out of the way in time, and the water, under pressure, hit me square in the face. I swear that I felt my eyelids lift away from my eyeballs. It was so hard and sudden that I backed up and stepped away from the pump. I was kind of blinded for a minute or two.

While I was waiting to regain my eyesight, I heard my partner's voice yelling nasty criticisms and condemning me for stepping away. What the hell else could I do? Hearing him just pissed me off. I screamed something at him that involved my desire that he do something unnatural and anatomically impossible in the hottest place that I could think of. Hmmmm...Maybe I did have something to say to him after all.

Old Homestead Fire

Ever since I was small, I remember my mother telling me that there had once been a fire in the house where I lived. It was an old house, the place where I grew up. It's on maps of the town as far back as the 1840s. Home inspectors have even identified some square, hand-hewn lumber and some reciprocating saw cut lumber that they said goes back to before 1825. In addition to being old, the house was cold and drafty.

When I was 22, my parents moved the family out of state and I took over the house. Taking the house was important to me then, for reasons I can't remember. When the place was mine, I set out to do some work to fix it up a bit like Dad never did. That was a job that, ultimately, I very much regretted taking on. I never realized just how much work the place really needed.

On the upside, as I started to fix it up, things got interesting. I found long, hand-hewn beams and wall studs that consisted of small trees squared off on one side. You could see the axe marks. The beams were six feet long and so old that there was no moisture left in them. They were huge pieces of solid wood, but couldn't have weighed more than twenty pounds. There were other beams pieced together in sections and held together with hand-carved wooden pegs.

I also found evidence of a pretty bad fire. Above the kitchen and living room ceilings, I found heavy charring. They were completely rebuilt with rough sawn lumber and balloon frame construction.

I was told that my house used to be the main house on the property. The structure right behind it was converted from a barn to a two-family house, while another little house a bit further away had been a caretaker's cottage. Sometime in the past, the property had been divided and sold.

The guy who owned the house before my parents is just a name I've heard. I have also heard of his exploits. The story of the fire, as told to me, was that the guy had wanted to get free gas from the gas company. He dug up a gas pipe somewhere nearby, I guess, and proceeded to drill into it. Well, I guess he kept drilling, even though the drill got hot and sparked as he broke through to the inside of the pipe. Gas came out into the cellar and found an ignition source and blew.

My family lived in town at the time, and an uncle, who was then a kid, told me he was playing baseball across the street at the ballpark. He heard an explosion and when he looked, he saw flames leaping up from the place. A man I worked with for many years said that he had been playing ball with my uncle and told me the same story. The house was patched up and my father bought it when I was about four months old.

One day years back, I was nosing around some old records in an old filing cabinet in the basement of the fire station, when didn't I come across the old fire report for my house! It was a single page report, filled out by a dispatcher. It included a payroll list of the firefighters who responded. I knew many of the names. The department was all call men at that time—no full-time firefighters. Looking at the payroll, the total cost was thirty-seven dollars and fifty cents. Man how the times have changed!

My Man

As a firefighter, I worked very closely with the police department. We've always shared a building together. For a while, we were all together in a building that housed the fire and police departments, as well as the town hall. I guess it worked at first, but as the town grew, the police and fire departments grew and soon we outgrew the place.

The town hall moved to another location and we divided the place up for just the fire department and the police. We got to know each other and I can say that I have worked with some of the finest people who are police officers. I have also met some of the worst. I guess this is true of any group, but it kind of stands out in the emergency services.

When I first got on the job, there were still a lot of real old timers from the 60s. They were used to working in Hooterville. Then the town evolved and grew, and got to be just a touch bigger than Bugtussel. Now these older guys were mixed with other guys, young go-getters that came on in the 70s.

There was one guy I remember. I don't know just when he came on the police department. He was younger than the old guys, but he was different. For one thing, he had grown up in town, something that few since then can claim. He was a pretty good guy, but best not to underestimate him.

My sister had a chance to meet him. I remember at one time she had some guy from where she worked start to get a bit too friendly. I think his name was Ted. He came to her house several times and tried to force his way in. My sister called me and I called the police, and who came? The cop in the story! He was a sergeant and he came out, but the creep was already gone. My sister was given his card and told to call him if that guy ever came back.

She didn't have to wait long. She heard a noise in her living room, went to see, and found the creep halfway in the window.

Now my sister was no shrinking violet. She got a frying pan from the kitchen and slammed his head with it. Then she calmly called the sergeant, who was there in the blink of an eye. The creep was still shaking off an overdose of frying pan when he was arrested. I don't know the outcome, but I know we never saw that creep again.

Holy Shit

The town that I grew up in had everything I could want. We had a school that I walked to and went home for lunch, a town beach, a supermarket, a post office, a bank, a pharmacy, and a library, all in easy walking distance from home. It was a great place to grow up.

For the grownups, the town also offered something else in the form of a neighborhood tavern. I think that the term "tavern" is pretty accurate. The place was clean and had a very good menu to offer, and being right on a pond, the scenery was pretty nice.

But the place had gone through some big changes in past years. Not so long ago, calling the place a "tavern" would not be quite right. It was a bar, plain and simple.

The bar has an interesting history. It started out as a speakeasy during the 1920s. Back then, it was almost wilderness out our way, and the pond was surrounded by little dirt roads cutting through the trees around cottages for sale or rent. People spent their vacations there.

This was all before my time. I remember the place as a private club you needed a card to get into. My father and uncles were all members, and sometimes, when we were water skiing in Dad's boat, we'd slip inside after we took the boat out of the water. Dad and the uncles would keep me full of cokes and let me play a bowling game while they drank their beer. The place was clean then, too. There was sawdust on the floor and the tables were clean.

Later, when I got old enough to drink there, the place started getting kind of dirty, but that didn't apply to the men's room. That room was positively filthy. The urinal was a trough that was always filled with coins for the desperate person to pick through if they needed a drink that bad. The toilet stall was made of plywood with no door, and everybody knew that you didn't sit down there, if you knew what was good for you.

I haven't drunk for many years now, but I used to hang out there regularly. The food wasn't bad either, but the attraction was the booze. People watching can be fun, but in a bar where everybody is half in the wrapper, it can be hilarious.

The bar was well-known throughout the area and beyond, and did a very good business. One of the people making business so good was a town selectman. He lived in the south end of town and was known to frequent that bar. He'd been in local politics for many years and was well-known in town.

I remember one time I was in there in the late afternoon. The place was busy. After a while, people started noticing a terrible stink that was coming from the men's room. A few cut their way through the stink to see what the problem was. There, on the throne, sat our town selectman, thoroughly intoxicated. He was wearing a suit, like he always did. There wasn't much room to move around in the stall, but somehow the man managed to cover himself with shit. It was in his hair, on his clothes, and on his hands. It was even on the walls of the stall. There he sat, trying to clean himself up.

I don't know how he made out. I suppose they got him home, though the ride was sure to be aromatic. They didn't ban him from the place and no one ever said anything about the incident, but he had to be embarrassed to show his face for a while. After all, he was a duly elected town official!

Time Marches On

I'm now in the fifteenth year of my retirement from the fire department, after thirty-three years of service. I left the fire academy nine years ago after twenty-five years of helping to train firefighters, mostly in the recruit program. Except for the administrative people, everyone at the academy was a firefighter somewhere or a retired firefighter. I worked at the academy on my days off from the firehouse and I spent it playing with fire and firefighters. I loved the place and I found my place in teaching. I loved the job.

I continued at the academy after retiring from the fire department, still per diem, but I worked a lot of time there. I just can't imagine all the faces I've seen over the years, both staff and students. Some of them I've known from before I started at the academy, others gained a certain notoriety that makes them memorable. I had students that I would have worked with in an instant, and others that I was glad I never had to work with. There were the probies from around the state, as well as my own town and others from surrounding towns that I would come to know over the years.

I was just scrolling through social media when I came on an announcement of the retirement of a guy I knew from a neighboring town. I helped teach his class during his recruit training. He was a recruit along with two other people from that town.

I knew one of them. He was a guy I knew from the ambulance business and I had a lot of respect for him as an EMT and as a teacher of EMS. As for the fire service, he had grown up in it. His father had worked his career in the same town and had retired as a deputy.

The third guy was a very quiet, older guy. He would do his job and then some, and just smile. The people at his department liked him, so I guess he was doing his job.

The guy who started this story was someone I didn't know back when he was a recruit, but I would get to know him early in his career. His class had graduated and I hadn't seen him for a while during a time when I was having some personal problems. My wife and I had split up and I was driving a real piece of crap with a broken gas gauge. I got it fixed, but it broke again. Things like that never happen unless you're driving and then you only find out when you run out of gas.

Well, I did, and it wasn't the first time, either. I carried a small gas can and started walking. Soon, a pickup truck pulled up alongside of me and when I opened the door, it was him. He asked what had happened. I told him and he said he was glad to help me. While riding to the gas station, we talked. He was new on the job, so he had to buy his uniforms.

His department gave each firefighter a check for a certain amount as a clothing allowance. Out of that check, he had to buy uniform shirts, pants, shoes, coats, plus his bunker gear. His department only issued new hires a helmet and a flashlight. The rest had to be bought with the clothing check or out-of-pocket money. So he shopped and bought what he could, but on the day he picked me up, he told me that he needed a couple of other things and didn't know how he was going to pay for them. Clothing prices were going up and turnout gear prices were also very high. He didn't have the money to spend on a pair of boots.

At that time, my department had just issued a different style of turnout coat, one that used short boots and bunker pants, and no longer the old three-quarter boots that his town was still using. I had a pair of them that I wasn't using any more, so I offered to lend them to him. He lit up and thanked me profusely. I got some gas and he drove me back to my car.

The next time I was on duty, he came by and picked up the boots with a promise to return them when he got his next clothing check and could afford his own. Those boots were like new and he put them to good use. I knew he must have gotten another clothing check when one day I found my boots waiting for me in the firehouse, all clean and dry and put away on my rack.

Many years later, the boots came in handy again. Friends of my wife in NYC had a vacation home right on the beach. The house was on stilts and the water often came up under the house. The husband had to do some maintenance work under the house where it was always wet. He told me about that and he asked me if I knew where he could get some boots like mine. I said that I had a pair I wasn't using that he could have. He was ecstatic. I mailed him those boots, and soon after, they sent me a picture of him wading in the surf with my old boots on!

Why am I writing this, you ask? I read the retirement notice. It said that the lieutenant was working his last shift after twenty-eight years.

A couple of summers ago, there was a Meet and Greet at a firehouse where there was another man who worked with that guy since he was a recruit. In fact, I took that man's class picture when they graduated from the academy. It was his camera and his tripod, but I snapped the picture! That man was a very well respected firefighter and instructor, both in his department and at the academy. He had risen to the rank of deputy and was retiring. I was out of town, so I missed the Meet and Greet and I regret that, but here were two men who I've known right through their whole careers and now they're retiring. Holy Shit…I'm Old!

Some Thoughts

Back almost fifty years ago I decided to give the fire service a try. I had known several friends whose fathers were firefighters and it seemed like it would be fun. The department in town was going to hire some call men and the job came with some academy training, too. I decided to give it all a try--and never looked back.

I put in thirty three years as a firefighter/EMT and twenty five years at the fire academy, helping to teach new firefighters the craft. I've been retired now from the fire department for fifteen years and from the academy for nine years. I have a collection of memorabilia scrapbooks and so many memories, but most importantly, now I have the honor of saying : I am a retired firefighter, the best job in the world!

Glossary

10s and 14s
Once a common shift schedule consisting of 10-hour day shifts and 14-hour night shifts

24s
Common shift schedule consisting of 24 hours on duty at a time

0200
2:00 a.m. in 24 hour time

0230
2:30 a.m. in 24 hour time

1700
5:00 p.m. in 24 hour time

1800
6:00 p.m. in 24 hour time

academy
See Massachusetts Firefighting Academy

all-call department
A department consisting of part-time workers who are called in when needed

altered mental status
A person who is not behaving the way they normally do

bunker gear
Protective clothing for firefighting (helmet, hood, coat, pants, boots, gloves)

burn building
Concrete building at the Massachusetts Firefighting Academy designed for live-burn training. It can withstand multiple lightings of fires over years.

call man
Part-time firefighter who only reports for duty when called in to provide additional help for emergencies. In my town, they do not work regular shifts at the firehouse.

Capt.
Nickname used to address a captain

class A uniform
Fire department dress uniform worn for special occasions

day room
Room in the firehouse commonly occupied by firefighters when not engaged in duties or calls

Dep.
Nickname used to address a deputy

DNR order
A "Do Not Resuscitate" form filled out by a person indicating that they do not want any resuscitative measures taken if they experience sudden death

DPW
Department of Public Works

duty captain/officer
The commander of the shift

Emergency Medical Technician
Person with basic level of medical training (i.e. CPR, defibrillator, Epi-pen)

EMS
Emergency Medical Services

EMT
See Emergency Medical Technician

fire academy or **firefighting academy**
See Massachusetts Firefighting Academy

igniter
The person in charge of lighting the fires for training

incident commander
Person responsible for and in charge of all aspects of an incident

jump kit
Medical bag

LODD
Line of Duty Death

mask up
To put on the face piece of the SCBA

Massachusetts Firefighting Academy
The state facility that provides training for any firefighter in Massachusetts at no cost to the individual. Many towns send their new hires through the recruit program.

MFA
See Massachusetts Firefighting Academy

MFFA
See Massachusetts Firefighting Academy

OD
Officer of the day, duty officer

ready room
Instructor's room

recruit program
Training program at the Massachusetts Firefighting Academy for new firefighters to learn basic skills of firefighting

SCBA
See self-contained breathing apparatus

Section 12
Section of Massachusetts General Law detailing requirements for involuntary committal to a hospital for a patient with questionable mental status

self-contained breathing apparatus
Air tank, hoses, face piece, and all necessary parts of the breathing system worn on the back of firefighters and used in environments where they cannot or should not breathe the air

short timer
Person with only a short time remaining before retirement

state firefighting academy
See Massachusetts Firefighting Academy

step
Flat wide platform on the rear of an engine where firefighters stand (and hold onto an upper bar) while responding to a fire

strike the box
To have a box number sent through the alarm system, transmitted to the stations in town indicating that there is a fire at that location

trip a box
> To activate a fire alarm box to notify the fire department of an emergency at that location

turnout gear
> See bunker gear

vollies
> Volunteers

watch room
> A room, formerly used for the dispatcher, now used for greeting the public and routine business

well-being check
> Going to a person's house to check on their welfare at the request of family or friends who are concerned because they are unable to reach that person

www.ingramcontent.com/pod-product-compliance
Lightning Source LLC
Chambersburg PA
CBHW071430150426
43191CB00008B/1097